PAUL NICHOLS

SEX

CELEBRITIES

AND SPY CAMERAS

THE MEMOIRS OF A HOTEL NIGHT MANAGER

PAUL NICHOLS

SEX

CELEBRITIES

AND SPY CAMERAS

THE MEMOIRS OF A HOTEL NIGHT MANAGER

MEREO
Cirencester

Mereo Books

1A The Wool Market Dyer Street Cirencester Gloucestershire GL7 2PR
An imprint of Memoirs Publishing www.mereobooks.com

Sex, celebrities and spy cameras: 978-1-86151-791-3

First published in Great Britain in 2017
by Mereo Books, an imprint of Memoirs Publishing

The address for Memoirs Publishing Group Limited can be found at www.memoirspublishing.com

The Memoirs Publishing Group Ltd Reg. No. 7834348

The Memoirs Publishing Group supports both The Forest Stewardship Council® (FSC®) and the PEFC® leading international forest-certification organisations. Our books carrying both the FSC label and the PEFC® and are printed on FSC®-certified paper. FSC® is the only forest-certification scheme supported by the leading environmental organisations including Greenpeace. Our paper procurement policy can be found at www.memoirspublishing.com/environment

Typeset in 12/18pt Century Schoolbook
by Wiltshire Associates Publisher Services Ltd.
Printed and bound in Great Britain by Marston Book Services Ltd
Printed on FSC-certified paper

Dedicated to all those who are doing a job they
love and hate at the same time.

INTRODUCTION

This story could just as well be yours. I think I am a fairly ordinary man, so how I came to be in an extraordinary situation remains to be seen. Fortunately, it is my story to tell, and I'm about to share it with you.

My name is Paul. I'm single and a shade over six feet tall, with an athletic physique and an olive complexion, and I am thirty-one years old. Some people call me handsome, which is probably part of the reason I came to be in this situation, as you will see. Also, just for reference – and in case you are interested – I am a practising heterosexual. Practice makes perfect, after all.

I'm sure that at some point in our lives we have all

found ourselves in a job we have decided to do just for the money, even though we hated it and hated almost all the people we had to work with. But if you've ever been in this situation, I bet you carried on, if only for the money, as long as it was good enough. I bet you'd do it for the sake of paying for a skiing trip or for that sun, sea and cocktail-fuelled holiday which would fade from your memory as fast as your tan, if it wasn't for those embarrassing pictures you posted on your social network page. Well, OK – perhaps that's just me!

But hopefully, you didn't have to work with the sort of obnoxious people I met when I was working at a well-known five-star hotel in central London. I'll call it the Hotel Mannequin.

From what I could see, whilst attending the numerous interview stages for a job at the Mannequin, the hotel wore two faces: a sober, sophisticated face for daytime and an untamed face of vulgarity at night. But the thing I liked about this hotel, even though it was five-star, was that it wasn't one of those stuffy hotels that are stifled by pompous ignoramuses who speak with plums in their mouths and keep themselves tight-laced, pretending that 'sex' is a bad word, to be used only in the confines of their bedroom. On the contrary, as I would soon discover, this hotel was thronged with people who were all too keen to explore life. The visiting and resident guests were never afraid to use experimental non-prescribed drugs at leisure and during sex, and were not afraid to do unbelievable things in the public areas.

And there were other attractions that were far too good to dismiss. I'm sure you would be as intrigued and enthusiastic as I was if, during your interview, you were told that you would be paid over £34,000 per annum for a four-day week, you would meet and greet celebrities, enjoy fine dining whilst on duty and have the added perk of a cash bonus whenever set targets were met. Wouldn't you jump at an opportunity like that? Well, I certainly did. It all sounded too good to be true. And in the end, I discovered that it was.

However, my eyes were gleaming with the possibilities. The way I interpreted the contract, if I worked according to their schedule of four days per week, followed by four days off, it technically meant that I would only be working for six months out of the year, which was absolutely fantastic!

However, there is one crucial point. I would advise you, if you ever come across such an opportunity, to scrutinise the details and always consider that there is likely to be a hidden agenda behind the contract. Yes, that might sound mysterious and confusing, but in my case it was more a matter of what wasn't said and wasn't written in the contract that made this job the most hateful job you would love to do. I skirted over the small print. In fact, the small print didn't cover the half of it. The real dangers and concerns were not mentioned at all. I didn't think of the implications or look for the catch. It wasn't my own idiosyncrasy, I'm sure. When was the last time you read, in full, the Terms & Conditions on a website? Don't we all just tick the box and hope it's going to be OK? When we're eager for the benefits, and keen to get to the good stuff, we all say, 'Yes, well, whatever. Anyway, great! Let me just sign the contract and get the show on the road.' Or in other words: 'Never mind all that. Show me the money!'

If ever a job sounded too good to be true, my job at the Hotel Mannequin was it.

CHAPTER ONE

After signing my employment contract with the Hotel Mannequin, I was given a start date in two weeks' time. However, just three days later, I received a call from the Deputy Hotel Manager, Stephanie.

"Oh, hi Paul," she breathed. "I'm really looking forward to working with you. I can't wait. In fact, I was wondering..."

In a highly seductive voice, she started trying to persuade me to start work ten days earlier than we'd initially agreed. She was really persuasive. As she was my manager and I wanted to show her I was keen, it was really difficult to resist her request, because

Stephanie was one of those stunning blondes you usually only see on spring catwalks, except that she had enough curves to put most famous pop chicks in the shade. How could I say no?

"Tomorrow? OK, great! I'll see you then," I said.

I was also excited about starting sooner. Fantastic money, faster than I'd anticipated! What's not to like?

Because I had been asked to start work so much earlier than planned, the specially-tailored uniforms they had ordered for me were not ready yet, so I was given the opportunity to wear my own suits until they arrived. I saw an advantage in this. The first day at work would be all about me making a great first and lasting impression. So I had already thought things through before I even got up the next morning, prepared to impress.

I thought I would start by choosing a shirt. From my initial impression of the hotel, I thought a light pink shirt with a dark pink tie would be perfect. It would provide a striking flourish of colour against the backdrop of my dark Ralph Lauren suit and my tan Oliver Sweeney shoes...

As I told you, I'm straight, but I'm meticulous about how I look. And I always believe you feel more confident when you know you're wearing the right perfume and underwear. So, infused with Dior's

Fahrenheit and adorned in red, tightly-fitting Emperor Armani underwear underneath my designer suit, complemented by a nicely-branded pair of Paul Smith cashmere socks, I compiled my own catwalk creation for work. I nodded my approval to the mirror, well-satisfied with the job.

With all new jobs and experiences, there is some anxiety before you launch into them. That day, my emotions were reminiscent of my first date. I was excited and full of anticipation, but I was also wary and not quite sure what to expect. However, knowing what I did about this job, I was optimistic.

As I set off on my twenty-minute Tube journey to the hotel, I mused about Stephanie, remembering just how stunning she was and how flirtatious she had been since we'd first met at the interview. I wondered if it was all just for show, or would it be something worth pursuing? We would see.

I got off the Tube at my station, pushing through the evening crowds. With a sternly focused smile on my face, I made my way to the hotel, which took approximately ten minutes of brisk walking. This walk to work felt good. It was definitely a more vibrant area than I was used to in my previous hotel jobs, with a lot more personality than you would see on a walk in Park Lane or Knightsbridge. There was just so much to see in this area, and more to do. It was buzzing with life.

And death, as I was to discover in due course.

I could see the main entrance to the hotel, which was opposite an office complex that closed at 5:30pm. There were a lot of people around the door area, just standing in huddles. From the cameras around their necks I knew they were press photographers, either cluttering up the pavement, poised on their motor bikes or hanging out of ramshackle cars, massive lenses at the ready.

The scene brought back memories of working at another five-star hotel, where I'd had the privilege of making the acquaintance of the late Patrick Swayze when he was appearing in a production of *Guys and Dolls*. Patrick was always hounded by press photographer when he returned to his hotel apartment after the show, so he sought refuge with me and would sit with me in my office almost every evening. It was a very pleasant experience. I got to know him quite well and we would call each other by our first names. He told me all about his ranch in Texas and his life in general. During the six months he stayed at that hotel, in one of the private apartments, I came to admire his witty sense of humour and love his unforgettable vocal tones. He was gentle with words, and not brash in the least. If you met him, even if you didn't initially recognise him, you would soon be reminded of who he was by his unmistakable walk, or the pose from *Dirty Dancing* that seemed to characterise him. Patrick wasn't the type of celebrity who would create a scene for no reason. He would always address others respectfully, in a polite manner. But don't get me wrong – he wasn't a pushover and he would never take no for an answer. Nor would he settle for anything but the best. You always knew you were in the presence of a star.

I walked to the main entrance and was greeted by a smartly-dressed doorman, not overburdened by the usual outrageous top hat and gold-braided suit or greatcoat from the turn of the century that many hotels insisted upon. He was really elegantly dressed.

"Good evening, sir," he said in a commanding yet charming voice, as he opened the door for me to pass through.

"Thank you," I replied. "And a pleasant evening to you, too."

As soon as the door opened, my attention was drawn to an artwork in the lobby that towered at least one metre above my head. To the left of the artwork stood a modern oak reception desk, behind which two gorgeously-dressed, good-looking female receptionists and a handsome gentleman stood. I descended the marble steps which led from the main door to the lobby and approached the desk.

The male member of staff who was standing at the delicately-labelled concierge desk stepped forward with a respectful smile, saying, "Good evening. Are you attending one of the functions in the events area?"

"Good evening," I replied. "No, I am here to meet your Deputy Hotel Manager, Stephanie Edwards. She is expecting me. My name is Paul ."

"Ah. I will let her know you're here." He nodded graciously, walked back to the desk and made a call.

So far, so good. While I waited for him to complete his telephone conversation, I wandered towards his desk, taking in my surroundings. I had to suppress a slight flutter of nerves, but overall, I was excited and relishing the prospect of being part of this place.

The lobby was carefully decorated with a few architectural plants, but no flowers. That made sense to me. From the research I'd done on this hotel before I applied for the job, and from what I had seen on my interview visits, it was clear that the hotel's client base was primarily middle-aged, and it was very busy: clients didn't have the time to stop to appreciate nature or enjoy any of the fragrant, decorative benefits of freshly-cut flowers in the lobby.

In most hotels it's customary to have lounge

seating in the lobby, where you would frequently find inquisitive guests pretending to read newspapers or magazines whilst really spying on other guests arriving, hopeful of spotting a celebrity. This hotel had none of that, enabling discretion and straightforward business. The lobby was just an open space, with the odd solitary plant starkly placed on the wooden floor and striking artwork on the walls, against a backdrop of stunning wallpapers and wide glazed windows.

The man at the concierge desk hung up the phone handset, looked up and said, "Ms Edwards is in a meeting and will be out very soon." I nodded my acknowledgement. He continued, "She said you can wait in the restaurant or bar in the meantime."

"That's fine."

"If you'd like to follow me..." He ushered me over to the restaurant. As I followed him and we passed other staff, I sensed curious, piercing stares digging into my back.

The restaurant was very busy, which is normal for a five-star hotel located in the heart of the city. When we arrived at the waist-high desk at the restaurant entrance, my guide whispered something to a lady standing there, presumably the hostess, while I awaited further instruction. The hostess came over to me and greeted me in a curious manner, her eyes speaking volumes, except that I couldn't interpret them.

"Good evening," she said. "My name is Anna. Let me show you to your table." She turned and headed into the restaurant, saying, "Please follow me," and whisking a menu off the desk as we went past.

Not far away, just to the right of the desk, we stopped at a table set for two. She pulled out one of the chairs and gestured for me to take a seat. As soon as I sat down, the menu was placed on the table in front of me.

"This menu lists both food and drink," Anna pointed out. "Please take a look to decide what you'd like, and I'll pop back and take your order."

"No need," I assured her. "It's a straightforward decision. I'm here to work, so I'll just have a sparkling water, please."

"Of course. Thank you."

As she took back the menu and walked back to her station, I started to survey the restaurant, my eyes skimming over the bar area and looking through to the lobby, which I could still see, even from where I was sitting.

As I gazed around my new environment, it was clear that it would be a fun and interesting place to work. The staff all seemed startlingly attractive, as if they had been chosen for their aesthetic appeal, and the uniforms made a very strong statement. One of my main observations was that the male staff didn't wear ties, and the female staff didn't wear tights under their tightly-fitting black satin dresses. Also, the backs of their dresses were cut in a deep V that plunged below their shoulder blades, giving the appearance that they were not wearing bras, and certainly exposing more skin than you would anticipate. How interesting! Their dress style was like a very subtle tease.

Less than a minute after the hostess had walked away from my table, my water was served. As the waiter poured it, a crowd of at least thirty people burst through the lobby, all chattering amongst themselves, and dispersed into the bar, where they loudly ordered rounds of drinks and bottles of wine and champagne. Where did they come from? It was clear that they had not come from outside. Some of the group, at least, were evidently staying at the hotel – I could see their room key fobs dangling from their hands or pockets. I decided that they must have been attending an event or filming within the hotel, since they had camera gear with them and other props befitting a film crew.

How splendid! With a flutter of excitement, I stared hard, trying to see if I could recognise anyone famous in the group. As I looked closer, I saw that they were a real motley crew, a melting pot of eccentric humanity. There were flamboyant drag queens and other more conservatively cross-dressed transvestites; cosmetically-enhanced women with expanded boobs, inflated lips and tight faces; granny teens, and some celebrity wannabes. As diverse and outrageous a group of personalities as you could get within one small area, with just the right balance – or rather, off-balance – of alcohol. It spelled a recipe for conflict. But this was nothing abnormal – on any given night in this part of London, it couldn't get much more interesting.

To regain my sanity, I looked away from the outrageous crowd and focused on the other, less interesting, people in the restaurant and the now much busier bar. It was a real mixture of clientele. What kind of crazy antics were going to break out here? I had no idea.

"Hi Paul!" A familiar female voice broke into my thoughts. "Nice to see you again!"

I looked up and saw that it was Stephanie, the Deputy Hotel Manager, and another older but equally gorgeous female. You could see that this was a woman of high expectations, obviously attractive and sexually appealing without being salacious. Her dress style also showed that she had good taste, since it was a selective outfit of high-end clothing. But to be honest, and I must be, to me, what stood out most were her breasts. They were the size of grapefruits, and they were peering at me over the top of her low-cut blouse. Slightly stunned, I dragged my gaze away, got up out of my seat and returned the greeting.

"This is Paul, the new Night Duty Manager I've been telling you about," said Stephanie to the newcomer. The woman gave me a stern stare and said tightly, "Nice to meet you. We have very high expectations here. I hope you will meet them."

Before I could even reply, she had turned on her high heels and walked away, leaving Stephanie and me standing there. I had opened my mouth, about to speak to the woman in greeting and response, and it remained open in bewilderment.

"That was Dana Walsh," Stephanie explained. "She oversees the management of this property." She sighed. "Don't worry. You will be fine once you've proved you're as good as I know you are. And don't get frightened by Dana. She can be a Rottweiler, but..." She stopped and closed her mouth momentarily. "Never mind."

I raised my eyebrows and Stephanie smiled, almost apologetically. "Come on. Let me show you your desk."

She led the way out of the restaurant, through the lobby and back to the concierge and reception desk. I followed her, admiring the milky cream sweep of her neck and watching her curvaceous figure as she sashayed along on her high heels, swerved behind the desk and went through a wooden door, which led us into the back office, or staff operations room.

The back office operation was really busy. Stephanie whisked me over to the area around her desk to show me the stationery store and her workstation.

She grinned and then pointed to a second computer. "We're sharing a desk – that's your workstation and chair."

She pulled out a folder from her desk drawer and gave it to me, carrying on with her instructions. "Inside, you'll find your locker key, your PIN number to enter the building through the staff entrance, and the passwords and information you need to log onto the various computers and systems."

Despite the flirtatious smile, she was all professionalism and efficiency. She emphasised that I should concern myself with the technical side of the operations. "As I recall from your CV and interview, you used the same systems and software at your previous hotel, so I won't bore you with the details. I am more interested in making sure you understand the physical operation and know where everything is located in the hotel. And for that," she said, "we will do a tour of the hotel, where you can meet all the staff while they're working. And then, you'll start our formal induction training."

She handed me another folder which was labelled 'Hotel Mannequin Bible'. And for sure, it *was* a bible: it contained all you needed to know about the hotel, from Standard Operating Procedures, staff procedures and company policy to the building plan, fire evacuation procedure, emergency numbers and suspension forms. It also had information about the various artworks adorning the walls. It was a really comprehensive guide, from a management perspective, and a very good reference point, if and when needed. I was impressed by the hotel's professionalism – then.

"OK, then! Let's go!" She smiled, and we set off on our tour.

Stephanie started off by introducing the back-of-house staff – Claire, José, Agatha, Teresa and Ewelina – who were sitting at their desks in the office where we were standing, and telling me what they did. Then we went through the door and back to the reception desk, where I was introduced to Rita, Joshua, Kim and Susanna, then to the concierge desk, where I met Les, Carl and Marcel. Next I was whisked around the hotel, where I met over fifty staff members from the various departments, including the Head Chef, Robert Noir, and the Events Manager, Manuel Hardy. I could not take it all in – certainly not everybody's names – and it was exhausting, trying to concentrate and keep smiling and looking intelligent as I introduced myself to everyone we met and explained my experience to the more senior staff and managers. But it gave me a good insight into the hotel operations, the pace of the work and the high standards that would have to be maintained whilst I was in charge of the hotel.

As we did our walk around, Stephanie handed me a list of names. "This guest list is to be kept confidential," she informed me.

At the top of the list, the word 'VIP' was underlined. Some of the names jumped out at me: Cameron Diaz, Oprah Winfrey, Daniel Craig, Hugh Grant, Denzel Washington, Kimberly Stewart, Chris Rock, Dwayne Johnson...

"Wow!" I exclaimed, as I looked through the list of twenty or so names. "I saw the press photographer as I came in. Now I can see why so many of them are outside. I guess it's going to be a busy night for us, then?"

Stephanie smiled. "It's always very busy. Never a dull moment!"

Time had gone by so quickly since I had arrived –

a glance at my watch surprised me, for it was already 11:30pm. We had now finished our walk around and I had received sufficient on-the-job training to allow me to work on my own.

"So, that's about everything. I think you'll be fine from here on." Stephanie gave me a meaningful look. "Judging from what I've seen!"

She was referring to my conduct and competence on our walk-around. When a guest sees a female and a male member of staff, they almost invariably make the assumption that the male is the more senior. Consequently, when Steph and I had been walking around the hotel, a couple of guests had approached me with their concerns. So I had already dealt with two minor complaints, although it had been nothing complicated or challenging, and altogether scored quite low on the scale of things that can go wrong. One of the guests claimed that her air-conditioning wasn't working properly, and another wasn't satisfied with the colour scheme of her room! Stephanie had held back with an amused smile on her face while I handled the issues, but I could see that she was impressed.

As we stood in the lobby, looking towards the restaurant and bar, Stephanie began, "I think you'll be fine. So, unless you have any particular questions…" Then her phone rang. "Oh. Excuse me."

This particular phone was the manager on duty's mobile pager – basically, the duty manager's phone, carried by whichever manager was in charge of the hotel's operations at the time. It was a phone I would be carrying myself as soon as my training was finished and signed off.

It rang three times before Stephanie could manage to get the phone out of her holster and answer it. I could hear the urgent, panting sound of the caller's voice, but I couldn't hear what they were saying.

"OK, then. I got you," Stephanie said. "I'll send Paul." She clicked the phone off, and looked at me seriously. "It might be nothing, but it's worth checking out. Are you OK with just going to down the events area? Go into Cinema One and have a look to see if there's anyone inside."

"Sure," I said, puzzled.

She went on to say that a staff member had been walking along the corridor when she had seen a male and female going into the empty cinema. "But they haven't come out and it's been five minutes. The staff said she looked into the cinema, but she couldn't see them inside, so it's a little weird."

"OK," I said, brightly. "I'll meet you back here in a couple of minutes or so."

I left Stephanie in the lobby and descended the

stairs that led to the events area and the cinemas. As I reached the events area, I met a rattled female staff member who pointed towards the cinema door and said, "They went in there."

I raised one hand in acknowledgement. "Thanks."

The heavy, soundproofed cinema door was closed, but as I pulled on the door handle, I realised that it was not locked, so no key was required. I entered the quiet, hollow room, lined with thick blue soundproof wallpaper and fitted with soft, thick carpets. The overall design of the space was to ensure that any sounds projected from the front were amplified. I could clearly hear groaning and low muttering sounds coming from that area, as if there was a film still running very quietly behind the draped curtain that covered the screen at the front of the room, I could also see a slight movement from the curtain in front of the screen up at the front. As I got nearer, apart from a strange, rhythmic bulging in and out of the curtains, I saw that the bottom hem of the curtain was rucked up, bizarrely revealing two pairs of shoes pointing toe-outwards towards the cinema seats. I quickly pulled away the curtains to reveal who was behind it.

"Aaargh!" screamed a female voice. "What are you doing?"

In surprise, I stepped backwards. There was a

woman with her skirt hitched up over her waist, her underwear around her ankles and a red-faced man wedged behind her posterior.

"What am I doing?" I replied in a raised voice. "No need for me to ask you what *you* guys are doing! I am the Duty Manager! Who are *you*?"

The woman quickly pulled up her underwear, tugged down her skirt, took to her heels and ran to the door, leaving the male to explain himself. He was left to face up to the embarrassing situation of being caught having sex in the hotel's cinema.

"Sorry," mumbled the man, tucking himself in and making himself presentable.

"You could have booked a room," I suggested.

He smiled apologetically and shrugged. "I would have loved to, but she couldn't wait. She was quite fired up – fiery and wet – and she wanted us to be really quick, before she went home to her boyfriend."

"Wow!" I said, blowing out my cheeks in surprise. "I'm stunned. That's a lot of information." I shook my head in disbelief. "Maybe too much. But nevertheless, I hope this will be the last time we will have this kind of situation."

"Oh, yes. Definitely." He assured me it wouldn't happen again, and then introduced himself as David, saying, "I'm a manager at a local film company and she works for us." He shrugged, as if to say, 'What can do, you do?'

As if that explained everything!

"Right," I said, bemused.

I was fascinated by the encounter and wondered what they were thinking – doing that, there, then. Or maybe they were just not thinking at all. It seemed such a crazy thing to do.

Chatting politely about anything except what had just happened, David and I walked to the lobby, where Stephanie stood waiting. I bade David an amicable goodbye and he headed into our bar area. Well, I couldn't blame him. Who wouldn't need a drink after that?

I explained to Stephanie what had happened and she laughed. I joined in, a quizzical look on my face. "You don't seem too surprised!"

"Ahem…" Her eyes twinkled with amusement. "Well, we have had similar situations in the past."

Our conversation was broken by the ringing of the duty phone. Again, Stephanie answered. It was the switchboard, passing on information left by Kimberly Stewart's personal assistant. Steph looked at me pointedly, phone to her ear, and repeated the message as she was being told it. "Ms Stewart's PA wants us to know that they are on their way back to the hotel…

Right now?... Now... Within five minutes. So we need to get our security guards to push back the press photographer from the main entrance so they can enter freely."

I nodded. As Stephanie relayed the information to me, I offered to partner one of the security guards and cover the main entrance with him. It would be my first taste of 'action'.

"OK. Speak to Chris. Well, I have to do some work in the back office, now." Stephanie handed the Duty Manager's phone to me, saying, "Will you be OK?"

"Sure." I took the phone and smiled. Our hands brushed, and I felt an involuntary thrill of electricity.

Stephanie smiled a genuine smile that lit up her beautiful face. Damn, she was hot!

"If you need any help, give me a call," she said.

"Don't worry. I'm sure I'll be able to handle things," I reassured her.

"You do know the protocol, though – yeah?"

I nodded. She was perhaps afraid I might grab a photographer by the throat and swing him around my head a couple of times before flinging him into the gutter. From my understanding of the company's policy regarding guest security, we were not allowed any physical contact with anyone on our premises, including press photographer, any unwanted guests or visitors. The only time we could use our bodies at all was as a shield or barrier to protect the guest, and we could not get into fights. It seemed like common sense, for a hotel manager, especially in these days of litigation. Lay a hand on anyone these days, and you could be accused of assault and taken to court – if not to the cleaners. So it was best not to engage at all. It wasn't anything too different from other jobs I had been in. I was experienced, after all.

Chris, the security men and I had been standing at the main entrance for a few minutes when we saw a black S-class Mercedes Benz with tinted windows approaching the driveway. As soon as the car pulled up, right next to our feet, we opened the hotel's main doors and waited for the passengers to alight. Before we knew it, we were overwhelmed by the photographers and blinded by the glare from camera flashes bouncing off the car's tinted windows.

As the passenger door opened in front of me, there was an epilepsy-inducing barrage of flashing lights and camera clicks from the heaving mass of shouting, greedy bodies pressing forward. It would be pretty scary for anyone, let alone a young woman, and I felt a surge of adrenalin shooting through my veins as I stepped forward, prepared for anything.

I instantly recognised Kimberly Stewart, Rod

Stewart's socialite daughter, by her haze of golden blonde hair, her strawberry-red lips and her blue eyes. As she was stepping out of the car, one long, lean bronzed leg after the other, a man suddenly barged forward out of the shouting, pushing wall of bodies with his hefty camera, and Miss Stewart was almost knocked to the ground.

"Hey!" Instinctively, I thrust out my left arm to catch hold of her, simultaneously using my right to shoulder the man out of the way. Rude bastard! I was seething. This situation was getting quite dangerous, and the constantly pressing, noisy, flashing crowd was a terrifying assault to all the senses.

Another photographer launched himself forward, but I used my body to block him, enabling a clear passage for Miss Stewart to walk between me and the open car door, and to safely make her way into the hotel's lobby. By this time, her friend was getting out of the other car door, and some of the press photographer were crowding the front entrance doors, trying to get into the hotel and savagely elbowing one another as well as me and their 'prey'. They were completely out of control, like a crowd of drunken rugby players whose rulebook has gone out of the window. They would have cut one another's throats if it meant getting close enough for a best-selling shot.

Lights kept flashing, and the cries of "Kimberly, Kimberly! Hey Kim! Hey, Kimberly, love!" were deafening.

I was appalled by their animalistic behaviour and complete lack of consideration. They were harassing these two young women in a most terrifying way. Growing increasingly angry, I busied myself keeping them out, being jostled mercilessly from all sides, whilst the other security ensured that Miss Stewart's friend was able to walk into the hotel without too much incident. Still they cat-called and pushed and barged one another out of the way. It was all Chris and I could do to keep firm and steady on our feet. No wonder media photographers get punched and their cameras smashed!

I was a little worked up, to say the least, about the way the press photographer had behaved and I began to shout at them, enraged. "You're a bunch of animals! Get off these premises! Go on! Fuck off!"

They returned my compliments. "Fuck you!" and "Piss off, bastard!"

The good thing was that by now, Miss Stewart and her friend were inside the hotel, safe and well, with the reporters and photographers left firmly outside. The security and I went into the hotel, and I saw that Kimberly was waiting in the lobby, just about where

Stephanie and I had been standing for most of the evening. Fortunately, she was completely unharmed and quite unmoved by the altercation. She was probably used to it. Certainly she was more accustomed to screaming crowds of press photographers than I was, and seeing her looking mildly amused helped me to shake off my remaining anger.

She came over to me, smiling with genuine interest, and asked, "What's your name?"

"I'm Paul, Miss Stewart," I answered, with a wry grin.

"Thanks Paul! You're our hero!" she breathed, a seductive smile playing on her lips. I could smell alcohol on her breath, but that was not unusual in our guests late at night – and they had been out clubbing, after all. "Can you please take us up to our room?"

"Yeah, Paul," said her friend, coming up close to me and fingering my lapel. "*Take* us."

Stepping into position on either side of me, the two women slipped their hands through the crooks of my arms and led me to the lift, leaning into me, giggling and chattering. While we were in the lift, I was aware of the overpowering smell of alcohol on both girls. *Whoa.* They had had quite a bit to drink. They started to sing and dance, lips pouting, heads thrown back.

They placed and replaced their hands on my chest, dancing as if they were pole-dancing around me, their legs straddling mine. "I love to make love to you, baby!" they sang.

I laughed in amusement, trying to mentally detach myself initially, but having two gorgeous leggy girls use you for erotic-dancing practice in a confined space, their hands everywhere, is not for the faint-hearted. For a moment, the blood rushed from my head to other places, and I forgot where I was and what I was supposed to be doing.

We reached their floor within seconds and they led me to Kimberly's room, 112. As I let her in, her friend, who was standing behind me, shoved me into the room. Before I knew it, I was slammed up against the bedroom wall and my jacket and tie were being taken off, while their hands ran up and down my body, long fingers teasing and squeezing, exploring gaps between buttonholes, skin and clothing. Things were getting out of control – in a good way – and I had totally lost any concept of my role as the duty manager.

At that point, unluckily (or perhaps luckily), my duty manager pager rang. Its harsh alarm brought me back down to earth, and I whipped it out (the pager, I mean).

"Awwww!" said the girls, disappointedly, eyes wide

in surprise. It was a sobering moment for all of us in the room. The screen showed that it was a call from the switchboard. My moment of madness seemed very distant as I took the call, resumed my professional demeanour and announced myself as "Duty Manager, Paul"

By then, both girls were singing again, quite loudly, "Baby, your fire is lighting me up..." and dancing across the room from me in a sexy and seductive manner, looking back at me smoulderingly over their shoulders, winking and beckoning to me with their nail-painted index fingers.

I quickly turned my back to them so that I could focus on what the switchboard operator was saying. I had to press my left hand over my left ear and squeeze the phone hard to my right ear to muffle their singing. I still struggled to hear what the operator was saying, but it became clear that the police were in the lobby and they needed to speak to the manager in charge. *Shit.* If anything was going to bring me down to earth with a bump, it was those words.

"I'm on my way," I told the operator.

"No Paul!" groaned Miss Stewart and her friend. "Oh, don't go!"

I grabbed my jacket and tie and waggled my finger at the girls, saying, "Naughty, naughty!"

"You have to stay!"

They pouted and complained, while I hurriedly made myself presentable, opened the door and ran to the lift. My mind felt a little dishevelled too, but stepping into the lift, I gathered my composure as I descended to the ground floor. I blew a breath of air upwards, trying to cool my hot face.

As I got out of the lift and turned the corner to the reception desk, I could see two uniformed police officers in the lobby, looking serious.

"Good evening, officers." I introduced myself and asked how I could be of assistance.

"Is there somewhere we can go where we can talk privately?" one of the officers asked, sternly.

My heart sank. "Yes, of course," I said, in concern.

It was really late by now. The restaurant was closed and there was only a handful of hotel guests still in the bar. I suggested that we could go into the restaurant, since it was already closed up and would be completely empty.

Within a single stride of us entering the quiet restaurant, one of the officers said, "We are carrying out an investigation into a murder."

"A murder?" I gasped, in shock and disbelief, stopping stock-still.

"Yes," the officer replied, "A murder. Someone has

been killed near your staff entrance."

My ears started humming and everything closed in on me. It was as though the world had stopped spinning or I had been tossed into space, because I seemed to be standing somewhere without gravity and everything was as black as night. Was it a staff member? A guest?

I guess the thought of someone being killed so near to the hotel had shocked me into a waking unconsciousness, in a completely sobering way. It could have been one of my colleagues! And where had I been while this was going on? Almost allowing myself to be seduced by a couple of young celebrity guests!

Before I knew it, Stephanie had come to my rescue. Having just heard that the police were talking to me, she hurried into the restaurant with grim determination. She looked at the police officers' grave expressions and my white-faced shock, and her face fell.

"What's going on?" she asked, clearly worried.

"Are you a manager as well?" one of the police officers asked, as they directed their attention to Stephanie.

"Yes," she said, concerned. "What's going on?"

The officer went on to tell her, "Someone has been killed, very near your back doorway."

"Oh, my God!" Stephanie's hand flew to her mouth,

her eyes wide.

"We would ask that your staff use other exits and entrances for the time being, as that area has been cordoned off while our investigation continues."

"Of course," Stephanie replied, recovering her professionalism.

"We do have a favour to ask. We believe that your hotel might have captured footage of the assailant on one of its CCTV cameras – the one that covers the alley leading to the staff entrance," the officer explained. "So I wonder if you could help us by letting us see your CCTV recordings, please."

"Our IT department are the only ones who have access to our CCTV system, I'm afraid," Stephanie replied. "They won't be in till 7am."

She went on to tell the officers that she would take their details and make a note of the approximate time-span of the footage they were interested in, so that IT could focus their attention on that period.

While she handled things, with me sitting quietly there, I had time to reflect on my shift so far. Unbelievable! Could this job get any weirder? This was my first night at work, and all sorts of things had kicked off. But it was only a mild eye-opener for what was to come.

Just reading this, you might think I'd made it up,

or that it couldn't happen in present-day London. Murder, sex, deceit and violence – with celebrity action thrown in. All in the space of my first shift. You might find it hard to believe, but no – this was all happening at two o'clock in the morning, a few minutes' walk from Oxford Street.

We all made our way back to the lobby and bade farewell to the police officers. Stephanie and I went into the back office, muttering our disbelief to one another, before starting the administrative part of the Duty Manager's role.

"We need to complete all the sections of this report by the end of each shift." Stephanie gave me a thick document. It looked like an encyclopaedia! I opened it and flicked through the pages, expecting this to be a week's record at least, but no – none of the pages appeared to be repeated. It all had to be filled in, accounting for our regular checklist tasks with comments, our individual report, and all details of the shift. I gazed at it in wonder and disbelief. All this for one shift?

"Blimey!" I exclaimed. "This seems very... comprehensive."

As I flicked through the thirty-five pages from front to back, I felt a bit sick. Filling this in was an unbelievable amount of work to have to do on top of being on the floor, managing the staff and attending to incidents and guests' needs.

Yes. Attending to guests' needs – and if Kimberly Stewart and her friend's needs were anything to go by, this was going to be a really fun place to work!

Or maybe, judging by other recent events, 'fun' was not quite the right word. Fun does not equate with murder. There is no fun in 'funeral'.

As Stephanie and I went through the book, we started to chip away at the checklist. To my relief, I soon realised that the booklet contained more fluff and explanation than actual written work. The tasks on the checklist could be completed within five hours, without any distraction. As I familiarised myself with it, I came to appreciate that it wasn't just meaningless bureaucracy. It all had to be done, so that everything would be ready for the morning guests coming down for breakfast, and to enable an efficient and effective handover for the morning staff coming in on their shift to run the day's operations.

Before we knew it, 7am was upon on us and the morning staff had arrived. The Head of Housekeeping, Inez, came into the office. "Hi guys!" she said brightly, fresh as a daisy, in contrast to our own jaded exhaustion. "Just to tell you – I've checked all the areas.

I see the night cleaners have done an excellent job." The restaurant and bar, along with the private areas for dining and events were also prepped and ready.

As is customary in hotels, all the senior managers, including the director in charge of our property, Dana Walsh, gathered together in the General Manager's office for a morning briefing. In these meetings, we would effectively do a formal handover and discuss anything that had happened the day before or overnight, especially if there were any follow-ups to be done or issues of concern to be aware of that we needed to communicate to our colleagues.

It was my first formal briefing at the hotel and I wanted to look keen and alert, but after a demanding twelve-hour shift and a pretty bruising experience, I just felt deflated. Stephanie and I explained what had happened, including the murder investigation and the scrum we'd had with the press photographer.

Dana Walsh seemed out for blood. Her way of operating became patently clear – she seemed to address everything we said with a dissatisfied sneer.

"And you didn't have time to complete the full audit, Stephanie? I am not at all happy!" she muttered, shaking her head.

When I explained the situation I had come across

in the cinema, she snapped, "Well, how did that happen? The cinema doors should have been locked, not just closed!"

Her brusque manner and harsh tone reflected the venom of her words. Everyone was subjected to a tongue-lashing from her, with no exceptions. She found fault with everything that anyone had done, including the way I had dealt with the press photographer.

"You do not speak to them – let alone shout at them like a fishwife! You maintain decorum at all times!" she snarled. "Don't you know the protocol?" She looked at me like something she had stepped in. Her permanently dissatisfied expression – accompanied by her sharp tongue and lack of empathy and diplomacy – had turned a gorgeous woman into a creature of ugliness, inside and out.

"Professionalism!" she hissed, scanning the group of managers. "That's what we expect here!"

She sniped at each manager and member of staff present as they gave their updates. She demanded to know the smallest detail, and criticised every word or action that had been taken. And it went on and on. I couldn't believe it. I hoped she was maybe just having a bad day, but from the brief encounter I had already had with her, and the jaded expressions on my fellow managers' faces, I feared that this was her usual behaviour.

Eventually, the torture was over and it was time to head home, after sixteen hours at work. As I headed to the Central Line Tube station, my head pounding, I seriously wondered whether or not I needed the hassle that came with this job. But the upside outweighed the downside – the pay, for one thing. Come on, I told myself. I can do this job for six months – and the shift system means that in real terms, I'll only be working for three months! Let's just see how it goes.

CHAPTER TWO

After only four hours' sleep, a quick dinner, a shower and 45 minutes' journey on the Tube into Central London, I arrived back at work. The novelty of it all still excited me, even though Dana Walsh's bad temper that morning had taken the edge off my pleasure. However, as I entered my PIN and opened the huge metal door that led to the staff quarters, I felt positive that tonight's shift had to be better.

"Good evening," said one of the housekeeping staff, a slightly-built woman with a narrow face but large, expressive eyes.

"Evening. I'm Paul, the new Duty Manager," I

smiled. "What's your name?"

I chatted for a couple of minutes, then went on. I met a few more staff in the corridor along my way, and some others when I went through to the canteen to pick up a coffee. I always took the opportunity to introduce myself to any staff I came across, learning their names and roles and chatting to them about my experience and background.

As I walked through the events corridor, I glanced at the cinema door and smiled, reflecting on my encounter the night before. Then I made my way up the stairs to the main lobby and the back office.

Greeting the staff there, I noticed that Stephanie's handbag was already sitting on the desk we shared. Her workstation was all set up, with papers open on the desk as though she had started work much earlier and was already well into it and hard at it. I glanced at my watch. I wasn't late – if anything, I'd actually arrived early for my shift. She must be very keen and diligent.

I sat down, got my Night Duty Manager's checklist and started to chip away at it, doing the bits of admin stuff I could manage to do on my own. Before I knew it, thirty minutes had passed without me even noticing, and I was still absorbed in the booklet.

Blood suddenly rushed to my scalp, which was

prickling with a gentle pressure.

"Argh!" I cried out and jumped involuntarily. Someone was gently stroking my head!

"It's only me!" a female voice said, bursting into laughter. "No need to scream."

I spun around in my swivel chair. It was Stephanie, toying with me, her blue eyes dancing with mischief.

So I laughed, too. "I was well away there!"

"Nice to see you're so dedicated to your work!" she said smiling, a teasing look in her eye.

"Nearly as much as you are – evidently! What time did you get here? In fact, did you go home at all?"

She pulled out her chair and sat beside me at her workstation. "I had to come in early today," she explained. "Claire, the Restaurant Manager, called at the last minute to say she's sick and couldn't come in. So I had to cover for her."

"Oh, no!" I said. "Did you get *any* sleep?"

"Yes," she replied, "but only two hours." She exhaled deeply. "Oh, I'm shattered." Wiping her fingers across her eyelids, she gave me a weak smile. "But it's bad news for you, I suppose – since I've already done a few hours here, I'm only allowed to work until 2am. So you'll have to do the latter part of the shift on your own and attend the morning briefing without me. Are you OK with that?"

"Of course!" I assured her. "I'm an old hand now."

Steph nodded. I noticed how pale her face was, and saw the grey shadows under her blue eyes. She stirred something in me that wanted to take care of her, even if she was my boss. Even if she was an independent, strong woman who could look after herself.

I felt confident that I could handle things by myself. By the time Steph left, the bar and restaurant would be closed to the general public and most of the staff would have gone home. This would leave me time to carry out the main administrative or technical tasks before the other managers arrived to offer additional support.

"OK, then, I might as well get started," I said brightly. I got up, asking Steph, "Have you got the duty phone and the override key?" She passed them to me. "Any relevant or pressing information?"

"Just the VIPs, and the usual. But otherwise – no, shockingly enough, it all seems to be quiet on the western front so far," she said. Her eyes were definitely tired, those dark shadows underlying the light application of make-up she wore. And since she had sat down, her bubbly energy seemed to have deflated like a balloon.

"That's good, then." I grabbed my notepad and pen and set off to visit the departments to check the staffing levels and to gauge how things were going.

While I visited the restaurant, I thought I would cheer Stephanie up by making her a latte and hand-delivering it to her, so I did.

"Awww! Thank you!" she laughed in surprise. "That's so kind!"

She really appreciated it. I could see the glow in her and the full blush on her cheek. I would have loved to have sat and chatted with her, but duty called, and I had to dash to the front desk to meet a VIP guest from 20th Century Fox.

On the face of it, the hotel was as busy as it had been the evening before, with a similar mix and blend of people. There was a lot going on in every department, and the press photographer were still waiting outside, like the predators and vultures they were.

As Stephanie had told me to the evening before, I got out the VIP list and glanced through it. Along with those who had also been on the list the day before, there were several other very noticeable additions, like Rihanna, Peter Kay, Chris Rock and Paddy McGuinness. Wow, it looked like it was going to be a fun night! As I compared the VIP list against the hotel's overall occupancy, it was clear that twenty-five percent of the guest were celebrities. Oh, what fun! I was really going to enjoy working here. I already did.

I completed my checks with the departments, including the events areas, which were really busy with private screenings and other corporate events that were in full swing. I thought I would loiter in the lobby for a few minutes before heading into the back office to check on Stephanie. But before I could complete my walk across the lobby, I saw two uniformed police officers coming through the main entrance. Bugger, not another crisis! My heart sank again, memories of yesterday's shocking news streaming into my mind.

"How can I help you, gents?" I asked the officers as they met me at the reception desk.

"Good evening," said the taller one. "We're just doing some routine checks in the area..."

Phew! I must have visibly relaxed.

"So we've just come in to say hello," the shorter, fatter one finished his sentence, "and to have a look around."

"OK. That's absolutely fine," I replied, in relief. "For a minute there I thought we had another major incident like last night."

"Oh, no. We just like to pay courtesy visits to businesses during the evening, to gauge the atmosphere and tone of the drinking patrons and suchlike," PC Tall went on to say.

They asked if it was OK for them to use our toilet.

"Of course!" I exclaimed. "You're more than welcome. And if there's anything else you need – if you want a coffee, or mineral water, or anything to go, we'll happily provide that freely, as a courtesy."

They declined this offer and set off for the toilets. I waited at the desk to say farewell to them, thinking it wasn't worth popping back to see Steph until they had gone, but after I had waited ten minutes, they still hadn't emerged and I was getting a little concerned. I decided to go and check that everything was OK, but as I headed in the direction of the toilets, the two officers came towards me, ushering a gentleman in handcuffs!

I was shocked. Wide-eyed, I shrugged in bafflement and asked them what was going on. PC Fat stepped aside to talk to me, while the other carried on walking to the main entrance with the handcuffed male.

"As we went to use the toilet, we came across this man using what looked like cocaine," the officer explained. I swallowed hard, my mind whirring, while he went on. "After searching him, we found a reasonable amount of the substance on him."

I raised my eyebrows, too stunned to speak. This place never stopped! A couple of guests, seeing the man being escorted off the premises, stood in the foyer, muttering together, concerned.

The policeman continued: "So we carried out a test with our drugs kit and found out that it actually *is* cocaine – so we've got to arrest him."

"Good grief!" I said, shocked. What was Dana Walsh going to say about this?

"Don't worry, your hotel won't need to be involved," he said, as if reading my mind. "We've checked already and the man had only come in to use the bar – he isn't a resident."

"Oh, OK," I said, in relief. That would be all I'd need, to give Dana Walsh more fuel to add to the flames of her fury.

Seeing a uniformed police officer talking to me, some other guests had hesitated on their way through the foyer and stood around, joining in the speculation, murmuring behind their hands or openly asking staff what was going on.

"Goodbye," the officer said to me, adding wryly, "Thanks for giving us the chance to use your toilets." He then joined his partner and the male they had arrested, who were waiting in the car parked at the front of the hotel. As they drove away, the onlooking guests and staff were all curious, buzzing with questions and speculation.

"What's he done?"

"Why were the police here?"

"What's going on?"

"Should we be worried?"

It took me a little while to explain politely what had happened, making it clear that the person arrested wasn't a hotel guest and reassuring them that the crime wasn't related to our hotel at all. As I was explaining what had just happened to more of the staff, one of our VIP guests arrived – Peter Kay. In the case of a returning VIP guest of his calibre, it was standard procedure for the management to meet him and escort him to his room, so duty called for me. I approached him to introduce myself. But before I could say anything, in his wonderful strong northern accent he declared, "Eh! Who's *this* one, then? You must be new! I've been comin' 'ere for a long time and I 'aven't seen *you* before! 'Ave you been 'idin' under a table in the back? Eh? 'ave yer?" His jovial grin lit up the room. He playfully jabbed the air with one finger, winking at me. "You 'ave, 'aven't yer?"

His infectious laughter had everyone in the lobby laughing as well. I managed to introduce myself and offered him complimentary beverages. "You can have them in our bar or wherever you choose to enjoy them," I told him.

He smiled, saying, "Aw thanks, Paul, but I'm exhausted. I'll 'ave to pass this time."

He went on to tell us about his rehearsal for the Comic Relief Red Nose Day's TV production. He also presented us with a big box of Krispy Kreme doughnuts, a favourite with the staff.

"Oooh!" chorused the reception staff, delighted. Their eyes were fixed to the box, mentally selecting their own favourites through the transparent plastic panel.

"See?" laughed Peter. "I know the way to people's hearts – through a doughnut!"

He knew the way to Amarillo, too. But I didn't like to mention that.

During our conversation, my Duty Manager's phone kept ringing. I initially ignored it, but I couldn't do that for long. It was persistent. Eventually, I had to apologise and break off our chat to attend to a staff query about some request or other.

It was from Rihanna.

"Paul! We've got no more coat hangers. Or rails!"

Rihanna had arrived with her whole entourage during that day shift and was expected to stay at our hotel for seven days, while she was performing in concert. This was during the period when she and her then-boyfriend, Chris Brown, had their highly-publicised falling out. He was accused – and later found guilty in court – of beating her up, but at that stage, no one really knew what was happening between them, or what to believe. It seemed to be a tempestuous on-off relationship. Naturally, everyone was curious about her situation, so the fact that Rihanna was now resident at the hotel would provide a good opportunity to get the picture about what was going on, and whether or not there was a new man on the scene. That's what the press photographer thought, at least. And I must say, I was curious, too.

Rihanna was staying in an executive suite that had opulent en-suite facilities. Ever since her arrival, we had received additional requests from her personal assistants for various items: extra clothes rails, a steam clothes press, a room temperature of 30°C, and hundreds of clothes hangers. Had we known her requirements before her stay we would naturally have provided everything she wanted in her suite ready for her arrival, but no one had made these requests in advance, and no one in the hotel had anticipated her high level of need or the many requests her team would make after they had turned up. Now these sudden demands for numerous pieces of equipment and supplies had created high drama at the hotel, because we didn't have all the items they wanted to hand. It was going to take some initiative and thinking out of the box to get everything together immediately. Especially since they wanted them, in one PA's words, 'yesterday', even though the party had only arrived that day. I guess she was only emphasising the urgency, but that didn't really help matters.

After about forty-five minutes of telephoning around neighbouring hotels, we were lucky enough to identify a few who could lend us the items. Having achieved that, I would soon have the opportunity to go to her room to inform her team that our mission had been accomplished – and, hopefully, to finally meet her.

As the stuff started to arrive from the other hotels, I was just in the process of checking them to see that they matched our standards and our guest's expectations when I was approached by one of the hotel security guards, Chris, the one I'd had to assist in dealing with the press photographer. He raised his eyebrows like a signal, expressing concern, but trying to be discreet about it. "Can I just have a quiet word, Paul?" he murmured, jerking his head sharply as an indication for me to follow him.

I stepped out of staff earshot and he continued speaking. "Um… I've been reliably informed that a staff member from Housekeeping with in-depth knowledge of ICT has set up a hidden camera overlooking Rihanna's bed."

"What?" I gasped in disbelief.

"We will remove and destroy it," he reassured me. "As yet, I don't know who it is, but I'll continue to investigate until I find out who's done it and report back to you."

"Thanks, Chris," I said, my mind still whirling. The implications!

"It looks like the staff have been doing it for a while," Chris warned. "And they'll go on doing it in future, if we don't address this. In the past, he might have set up hidden cameras in the suite used by other celebrities."

"Christ!" It was shocking.

I couldn't get my head around who could have done it, but I could understand why. The media offer very lucrative deals for information on celebrities that could give them a unique 'scoop'. Knowledge isn't just power – it's money too.

Chris left me to ponder the implications. If word got out about this, it would ruin the hotel's reputation. No celebrity – and very few other guests – would stay here with the knowledge that staff were spying on them with cameras. The question was how to deal with this discreetly without creating unwanted alarm or publicity.

The fact that staff spied on guests was bad enough. But my wonderful job was to became even more interesting, and my later discoveries were to be more than anything I could dream of. More than nightmares were made of.

I focused on the job in hand. Having finished checking the borrowed items, and being satisfied with their quality, I took the opportunity to help the staff to deliver them to Rihanna's suite. Well, you have to, really, don't you? In the busy life of a hotel, there is very little rest for a manager in my role, since in most cases, understaffing means that managers are kept busy plugging the gaps. And Rihanna's was one gap I was more than happy to plug. Metaphorically, anyway.

I straightened my jacket and fixed my smile as we knocked on her door and waited. But when we were admitted to the suite, disappointingly, she was nowhere to be seen. She was locked inside the bedroom, shouting to someone at the other end of the phone. "Damn!" I heard her say, vaguely, but that wasn't really what I was after.

We dropped off the clothes hangers and rails, but Rihanna was still firmly ensconced, deep in conversation behind the closed bedroom door. I hung around, asking if there was anything else that was needed, checking with her PAs that everything was fine, scrutinising the room temperature switch and biding my time by making inane hotel small-talk. After a few moments of shuffling my feet awkwardly and smiling, until it was clear that Rihanna wouldn't be appearing any time soon, I got the message. Clearly I wasn't going to be able to wait around to catch a glimpse of her without looking like a very obvious and complete fan-boy, so I reluctantly left.

Feeling disappointed, I headed back to the back office, just in time to say goodbye to Stephanie. She was putting on her coat, ready to leave. I could see that she was deflated and tired; the usual sparkle in her eyes was gone. She was exhausted.

"Goodnight, Paul," she sighed wearily, managing to raise a weak smile.

I wished her good night and a safe journey home, and sat down to do some accounts and report writing. There were several accounts discrepancies and it took me a little while to resolve them. As I focused on crunching the numbers, Carl, the concierge, came in and said, "Paul, I have a guest, Ms Ellis, at my desk. She is staying in room 216 and wants to talk to the manager."

"Cheers. What's it about?" I asked.

"She says it's confidential."

"OK." I shrugged, and went to the lobby to see her.

Ms Ellis was a lady in her late twenties to early thirties, with lovely brown hair, about shoulder length. She was smartly dressed in a blue skirt, orange blouse and black cardigan. But her face was white, and she looked to be in shock.

As I approached her she asked me urgently, "Are you the manager?"

"Yes," I replied. "How may I help you?"

"May I speak to you privately?" she breathed, her eyes wide in fear. "I have a problem."

"Certainly," I said, wondering what could have rattled her so much. I ushered her away from the desk and towards the lift.

She started by saying, "I don't know you, and I don't know how you will feel about what I am going to tell you..." She sighed heavily and muttered, almost apologetically, "There is something inside my room."

"What do you mean?" I frowned.

She went on, "I'm not crazy, but..."

That phrase usually precedes someone saying something that is indeed crazy and thereby proving themselves to be crazy, so I braced myself as she continued."

"There's a negative entity with really bad energy in my room. Can you please come with me, to my room?"

Entity? She looked wild-eyed with fear. But whatever was scaring her, I was certain I could reassure her.

"No problem," I replied calmly. "Let's see how I can remedy this situation."

We took the lift together up to the second floor. She was clearly still afraid, wringing her hands and shivering involuntarily. When the lift door opened, she took a deep breath, then walked to her room. She gave me her key outside, her hands trembling, saying, "Can *you* please open the door?"

I started to think that there must be something in the room that had frightened her, since she was shaking so much and obviously overwhelmed with fear. I inserted the electronic key and turned the door handle. The guest stepped backwards, gasping, and hid behind me.

Now this was becoming a little too weird for my liking. I wasn't sure whether or not she had some mental health problems. Perhaps I should even be afraid of *her*, because her behaviour was so irrational, although she was petrified herself.

I stepped into the room first and Ms Ellis hesitantly followed, cowering behind me and practically tugging on my jacket. I walked midway across the room and stopped still. She stopped behind me. I could hear her ragged breathing just behind me.

I said, "It seems safe. I can't see or feel any strange vibrations."

Suddenly she screamed, "There it is!"

"Where?" I peered around the room. I couldn't see anything.

"In that corner," she pointed, whimpering, her hand up to her mouth. "Near the window – beside the nightstand!"

By this stage, I'd started to believe that she was joking or maybe had a hidden camera somewhere, collecting footage for some prank show. Or at worst, that she really was crazy. She hurriedly retreated towards the door, her blue eyes wide, practically out on stalks.

I said, "It's probably best if we move you to another room."

"No!" she said, frantically clutching my sleeve. "What would prevent it from following me to my new room? You have to get rid of it altogether!"

She was adamant that there was some kind of entity she could see in the room. I had to think something up quickly to reassure her, whilst not looking stupid or rudely implying that she was insane. Thinking on my feet, I told her, "I don't know much about these things, but I do have a member of staff who does."

"Do you?" she gasped in relief, a weight clearly lifting from her. "Can they help?"

"I'm sure he can," I reassured her. "In fact, I know he can."

She was so happy! Her whole body visibly relaxed, a great deal of the tension that held her together dissolving, and she almost smiled.

I said, "I'll call him up here, and we'll try to get rid of the spirit."

"Oh, please do!" she begged me, almost tearful.

I took out my radio and called Mokabi, a staff member who worked as a night cleaner. I wandered a few steps away from the lady, saying in a loud voice so she could hear, "Mokabi, can you come up to Room 216, and bring some candles, a bible and a small bowl of holy water, please?"

"What?" asked Mokabi, more used to handling floor polish and bin-bags. "Where am I going to get holy water?"

"Just water," I whispered, adding loudly for the benefit of the guest: "We need your help. I'll explain when I see you."

"OK" Mokabi said warily. "I'll be right with you."

I spoke calmly to the lady, trying to reassure her. "Don't worry. This will only take a few minutes and then everything will be fine."

"Do you get this sort of thing happening... a lot?" Ms Ellis quavered, her eyes darting around the room like a cornered animal.

"No," I said. "Do you?"

"Never," she said, her gaze imploring me to put her out of her misery.

Mokabi arrived, wide-eyed and questioning. My expression as I opened the door told him to shut up and go along with what I said. "We need to get rid of a bad spirit, Mokabi. I told Ms Ellis that you are very experienced in these things." I nodded pointedly at him, my eyes willing him to agree.

After a split second of bewilderment, he caught on. "Oh, yes, indeed," Mokabi enthused, nodding emphatically. I prayed he wouldn't over-act, but our guest was in no state to pick up on nuances of behaviour; she was too terrified.

"Ms Ellis, would you mind waiting inside the bathroom?" I asked. "It's just while we set up the items we will be using to get rid of the spirit."

She looked petrified, and didn't move.

"You will be safe there," I reassured her. "Shut the door."

She did as I asked. In a low voice, I briefed Mokabi to read a passage from the bible and then to say, "Get out of here!" in his native African language. I knew the guest wouldn't understand it, but it would suffice to imply that some sort of conjuring was going on. Meanwhile, the lady cowered in the bathroom, waiting for us to exorcise her dark entity. All the time this was going on, I wondered if I was doing the right thing. Were we playing with fire? What if there really was something evil in there? Would we provoke something that really would haunt us later?

I set up the candles in a pentangle shape, sprinkling some pretend 'holy water' around, and called the lady to tell her that she could come back into the bedroom area. She opened the bathroom door a crack and whispered, "Do I *have* to come out?"

"No. You can stay there if you like," I said. "I just want you to know that we're starting, and you can watch if you want to."

"OK." She tentatively stepped into the doorframe, still clutching the edge of the door tightly, her knuckles white.

I got Mokabi to read Psalm 91. "He that dwelleth in the secret place of the most High shall abide under the shadow of the Almighty..." he intoned, his deep voice booming with authority. Even I was impressed. He was wasted as a cleaner. "Thou shalt not be afraid for the terror by night; nor for the arrow that flieth by day..."

Our guest peered around the bathroom doorway, watching the proceedings from a safe distance, her eyes wide, flashing their whites. Mokabi finished the passage and closed the bible with a soft clap.

"ONDOKA!" he cried in a loud, rich voice that even rattled me. "ONDOKA!" He waved his hands with an elaborate flourish, for good measure. "Get away from here!"

A minute passed in silence. Mokabi and I raised our eyebrows expectantly, looking from one to another, and across the bedroom, waiting to see how Ms Ellis would react. She stepped out uncertainly, her eyes darting warily around the room. Then her face broke into a beaming smile and her whole body collapsed in relief. "Oh, thank you! It's gone! I can't thank you enough!"

"No trouble at all," I smiled politely, and left, taking our resident exorcist with me.

"Thanks, Mokabi," I said, patting him on the back. "Well done."

"Need me for anything else?"

"No. I think we've had enough 'exorcise' for today," I said, grinning. I had had to deal with the possessions of guests before, but this was a different kind of possession.

Mokabi and I went our separate ways, smiling and satisfied. Either he was a great actor, or a powerful priest. We couldn't tell which.

Talking about possessions, I don't go looking for it, but I have often come across confidential information left lying around bedrooms. Or displayed on the screens of laptops that are left switched on in the room while guests go to dinner. Naturally, it is none of my business – and part of the job, working as a professional in the hotel business, is discretion and diplomacy. But I suppose you have to allow for human nature: if someone comes across a document lying about, curiosity will often get the better of them and they just won't be able to resist taking a look. It's a bit like a sign that says 'Wet Paint'. People can't resist touching it, just to check. So your eyes are irresistibly drawn to personal items and correspondence if they are left lying around.

I think everyone would like to think that hotel staff are completely trustworthy, but I can assure you, from personal experience, that it's always worth being careful with your private belongings. Over the years, I have come across many situations in which staff have been caught going through guests' luggage, laptops and documents. Whether it comes down to curiosity, pure and simple, or whether they're looking for information or something that might be of commercial value, it happens.

Of course, 'just having a look' becomes more serious when information is actually taken from the room. Saving documents onto a memory stick or 'borrowing' papers to copy in the back office before returning them takes only a matter of minutes. You wouldn't believe the kind of information that can pass through the hands of devious back-of-house staff – but then again, maybe you would. Secretly 'borrowed' items can end up copied and passed on to scandal-hungry journalists – for a price.

But sometimes guests can be caught out in other ways, simply by trusting the discretion of staff when they ask for help with personal or professional administration. Extra copies can easily be made of any document that a guest has asked to be scanned, faxed or duplicated by our office – with one press of a button. And the things that can happen to this stuff are unbelievable. Anything – from people using hotel guests' business and banking details to steal money to revealing personal information and selling salacious stories to the tabloids. Even blackmail. Anything goes.

For example, stand-up comedian and actor Chris Rock was undergoing divorce proceedings, and one staff member was caught photocopying and scanning his child custody agreement document, ready to send copies to the press. The staff member was seeking to make money out of whatever information they could glean from the confidential details of his custody case. Personally, I had never seen anything in the media about Chris Rock's personal situation, so I was unaware that there even was an ongoing custody case. However, newspaper hacks had several staff members in their pockets, who were always on high alert for snippets that could make the headlines with the aim of making themselves a handsome profit.

The Mannequin Hotel was a microcosm of all that was bad in the world – and, as far as my opinion of Steph was concerned, all that was good, too. But on balance... well, I'll let you judge for yourself.

And then there was the incident of the woman who claimed to have been raped by another guest...

In the tea lounge one night, at about two in the morning, two guests were having drinks and flirting outrageously in the otherwise empty room. In fact, with every drink, their inhibitions were increasingly discarded, and the male was openly fondling the female guest. Had the staff not been present, still serving them from the bar, and had they been alone, they clearly would have been taking things further, there and then. They were all but having sex, to the staff's discomfort.

"Do you think we should say something to them?" asked Elana, one of the bar staff, her eyes fixed on the man's hand, which was cupping the woman's breast, his fingers tweaking her nipple. Meanwhile, the woman was apparently slipping her hand up his thigh.

"I dunno," John, a waiter said, shrugging and pulling an uncertain face. "It's our word against theirs. I suppose they could justify themselves by saying they were only kissing."

"Kissing? They're practically devouring one another!" Elana said. "And his hands are all over her."

"It's embarrassing," agreed John. "But I don't think it's quite bad enough to say something… just yet. We'd probably end up in trouble for pissing off guests."

"Well, if any clothes come off, I don't care, I'm calling one of the managers to deal with it," Elana muttered, wiping a glass more forcefully than necessary.

"Oh, you Roman Catholics!" smiled John.

"Oh, you gay boys!" Elana snapped back, good-humouredly. But as her eyes strayed back to the couple, she shook her head in disbelief.

After several drinks, the couple went up, evidently to the lady's room, giggling conspiratorially and kissing one another passionately.

"There," said John. "We didn't have to tell them to get a room after all!"

After a couple of hours, we saw the man leave the female guest's room and returned to his own. All seemed well. But two hours after that, the lady telephoned down to reception, clearly distraught. She sobbed, "Oh, please! You have to help me! I have been raped!"

Obviously concerned, I quickly went up to her room and she tearfully explained that she had been raped by another guest. She said that she had met him in the tea lounge, but she didn't know his name.

Whilst we were talking, her laptop buzzed with a Skype call. "Oh, it's my boyfriend calling from the States!" she squealed, bursting into tears. "I have to speak to him." She lunged over to reach for the call button. "Eric," she sobbed, answering the call. "Oh, my God!"

I tactfully left the room to allow her to explain the situation to her boyfriend, while I called the police.

The police arrived soon after, and while they interviewed her, I carried out my own investigation to find out who the male guest was. It didn't take much doing.

John, who had been serving them drinks, said,

"She was with the male guest in Room 27. But *rape*? Honestly, they were practically shagging one another in the tea lounge, and there was no coercion there. We thought we might have to have a word with them, it was so bad. But then they left together, anyway. Couldn't seem to wait any longer!"

"Practically eating one another!" added Elana. "I thought it must be a very new, passionate relationship. I guess we should have known that they weren't actually partners."

Having found out that the man in question was staying with his own girlfriend in Room 27, I telephoned up to the room and discreetly asked him to come down to the front desk so that we could clear up the allegations. He was a little puzzled, but he came willingly, since he didn't want his girlfriend to find out what had happened.

He still looked bewildered when he arrived in the lobby, his hair dishevelled with sleep. And exertion, no doubt. As the police explained their investigation to him, his face became ashen with shock when he heard the accusation.

"Oh, my god!" he exclaimed, in absolute horror. "Rape? No way! The only thing I'm guilty of is cheating on my girlfriend!" He leaned forward, glancing shiftily from side to side to see who was around, and lowered his voice. "Look, I really don't want my girlfriend to know I slept with someone else. Can we keep this quiet?"

"That depends, sir," said the police officer, frowning. "These are very serious allegations."

The man looked momentarily blank. Then, as realisation dawned, taking in the implications at last, he gasped, "Oh, God, I feel sick!" He looked helplessly at each of us in turn, wild-eyed.

John and Elana were briefly interviewed to explain what they had observed in the tea lounge. Although the couple had had a few drinks, they assured the police that the lady hadn't at all been drunk and incapable of making an informed decision. She had certainly appeared to be a willing partner.

The police spoke to the alleged victim again, explaining their findings so far. In the end, appalled to hear other people's evidence and observations, the woman broke down and admitted that she'd made up the allegation after an attack of guilt.

"I felt absolutely terrible afterwards! And Eric was planning to call me. I just didn't know what to say."

She regretted that she'd been unfaithful to her boyfriend and had desperately looked for an excuse for what had happened. This seemed quite crazy – her boyfriend was in the States and wouldn't have known anything about it. The police were not well pleased. Nor were we, to be fair. But it was a relief to have the truth in the end, and we were all glad that she had decided to be honest. Well, as far as it went.

"I'm so sorry," She cried, begging us, "Please don't tell my boyfriend!"

I just don't know why she decided to make these accusations, even telling her boyfriend she'd been raped. Maybe he had tried to contact her earlier, before she'd rung down to reception, propelling her into a remorseful panic. I don't know. But she had wasted a lot of people's time, and – as it turned out – destroyed a couple of relationships in the process. No further action was taken against the male. But it was a very awkward situation on all sides.

It was fascinating to see what happened as a result. The male guest ended up checking out a whole day before his girlfriend, who had no doubt had more than a few questions to ask him, what with him being dragged from their bed to be interrogated by the police in the early hours of the morning. I can only assume that they broke up.

Since the woman he'd had sex with was staying in town on business, she remained at the hotel for a few more days afterwards. But following the events of that night, she had developed a tendency to leave and enter the hotel with her head held firmly down, a curtain of hair covering her face, and she never made eye contact with any of the staff.

CHAPTER THREE

While I was concerned about being efficient and professional in my role, Stephanie, as my boss, managed to handle all her responsibilities with good humour and charm – something that was sadly lacking in stone-hearted Dana Walsh.

Stephanie's duties were to act as Hotel Manager in the absence of the General Manager. This included some wide-ranging responsibilities, which she carried out most effectively, and without complaint. She oversaw the management of budget revenue and expenditure, including managing the monthly salaries and bonuses. She also handled the recruitment of new managers and supervisors, liaising with Human Resources to ensure that the hotel had adequate staffing levels. She would conduct departmental meetings and disciplinary procedures, and she designated staff cover, or provided cover herself, for absent managers in various departments. She was incredibly busy, but she always had time to offer me a radiant smile and a kind – or flirtatious – word, in spite of her challenging schedule. Her duties also meant that she managed all the daily operations of the hotel. And what daily operations there were at the Hotel Mannequin!

Quite frankly, I didn't know what the hotel would have done without Stephanie – or rather, what I would have done without her. She certainly made my work life more pleasant, and if I could have had my way, she would have made my love life more pleasant, too. But we would see. All in the fullness of time…

As for working at the hotel, the bizarre occurrences just kept on coming. I'd never known anything like it. There was one uncomfortable situation that I recall involving a gay guest and a male room-service attendant. The guest had called for a meal to be brought up to his room. The room-service attendant, Lukasz, brought his food, rapped on the door, and was told to 'Enter'. As Lukasz, entered the room with his eyes lowered, concentrating on steadying the tray, the guest said, "Can you bring the tray over here?"

"Certainly, sir." Lukasz looked up and did a double-take. The guest was sitting naked on his bed, masturbating languidly.

"Oh! Sorry sir," Lukasz spluttered, in embarrassment. "I'll come back later."

"No, no," the guest replied. He rolled his tongue over his lips lasciviously, still lazily stroking his cock with one hand, and grinned. "I'd like the tray and you over here, on the bed next to me." He patted the mattress beside him, his eyes widening meaningfully, nodding and smiling with an unnerving leer on his face.

The attendant dumped the tray on the end of the bed unceremoniously and ran out of the room. He ran all the way downstairs and into the back office, and in a tumbling rush of words, he complained to me, panting breathlessly with exertion, panic and fright.

"Thank you, Lukasz," I reassured him. "I'll deal with it."

"I'm not even gay!" Lukasz gasped, affronted. "Do I look gay?"

"I don't think it matters to some people, Lukasz," I shrugged. "You're a good-looking guy."

As we all were. Just as the girls were all beautiful.

I think it was an unwritten part of the 'essential criteria' in the person specification for any job role at the Mannequin Hotel – 'must be a head-turner'. It was all part of the hotel image. An image that was often superficial. Immaculate on the surface, but rotten beneath.

Of course, after Lukasz's unfortunate and unwanted proposition, I had to get Marc, one of our security staff, to speak to the guest in question and ask him to explain that his behaviour was unacceptable.

"He just laughed," Marc reported back. "The guy simply thought it was funny and said, 'Where's your sense of humour?'"

"Wanker," I muttered.

"Lukasz can vouch for that."

This overt and sometimes outrageous sexual behaviour wasn't always just an issue restricted to the guests, though. The thing about working in hotels is that it is all too tempting to have extramarital affairs. Everyone is friendly and sociable and it's easy to discover common interests. You have access to alcohol, beds and the choice of everyone working there, ranging from the over-sexed to the lonely or the desperate – male or female. Hotel Mannequin was no different from any other hotel in this respect. Think about it: most of us spent more time at work than we do at home. If you came across someone you clicked with, it was so incredibly easy to let it blossom in one of the bedrooms when no one else was around.

I used to fantasise that Steph and I might take our friendship further. I discovered that she had a partner, which was a slight dampener. But she was always so flirtatious with me that she signalled obvious availability. I wasn't interested in a quick screw in the laundry cupboard, though, behind her boyfriend's back. If I'm honest, I wanted more than a one-night stand with her. Knowing that she was living with someone, I kept a wary eye open for signs that she felt the same as I did. And I saw some, too. Yes, a hotel is a hotbed – literally – of illicit sex.

I once encountered a situation in which a male room-service staff member, Brad, was missing for two hours. I say 'member' purposefully. As became apparent.

"Jeez!" I was exasperated. "Where the hell is he?"

We had looked almost everywhere. It was a very busy period for the hotel, and Brad should have been delivering room-service trays to the guests' rooms, but no one could locate him. After an extensive search of the hotel, he was eventually found in a storage area, having sex with a woman who worked in the Housekeeping Department. Talk about 'missing in action'!

In an ideal world, staff who behaved like this would have been sacked, or at least suspended. It wasn't just misconduct – these employees were effectively stealing time from the company by having sex on work time, and failing to make themselves available to fulfil their duties. But the hotel was far too busy for us to carry out any suspensions: we couldn't afford to be understaffed. So, although they were both given a written warning, they otherwise went unpunished, on the understanding that their behaviour was unacceptable and should never be repeated.

The hotel was just far too busy for us to linger long over latest incidents. We just had to move on – we were swept along anyway.

The hotel was often booked for promotional events, including press junkets, media events at which distributors and publicists would promote feature films and the like. The campaigns would usually involve a mixture of press releases and interviews, chat shows and other TV and radio promotion, web-releases, viral advertising, merchandising and product campaigns. But we were generally and primarily involved in providing the venue for interviews with the makers and stars.

Once the hotel space was booked, a stream of people from the media and advertising world would be invited to interview the director, producers, actors or musical talent, to promote the film, or the album, if it was a musician or band. This interview process was the climax of a press junket – a chance for the stars to be photographed, asked questions and quoted in the media – and if it was part of a worldwide campaign, the budgets for these events could be huge. Bedrooms or suites in the hotel would be transformed into TV interview rooms for each of the major players, and elsewhere in the hotel, there were special press screenings and promotional rooms for the new films being released. It was a non-stop, exhausting process, with groups of reporters and interviewers moving from one room to another, interviewing individual stars, directors or producers and previewing films and videos. It was a hectic, busy schedule that had to be choreographed like a complicated dance, involving many participants in many areas of the building.

Meanwhile, the stars themselves and the directors and producers participating in this promotional marathon had to be protected from the pushy press photographer, handled carefully, given breaks from the media attention, and generally cosseted to keep them sweet. There was high pressure for everyone involved, and it was our role to ensure that everything ran smoothly and calmly.

It was perhaps no surprise then that after these exhausting, intensive, high-tension campaigns, the culmination of several months' work, the production company staff would later use the rooms to have wild, drug-fuelled parties to let off steam. While all this was going on, it was down to the hotel staff to somehow maintain a professional front and handle the room turnaround for whichever events were coming up next. Hollywood careers could be made or lost at these parties, and I know several people who got their big break in acting from simply being there – being seen, talking to the right people, flirting with the right people, and generally selling themselves – in one way or another. You had to be careful, though – you might unintentionally end up in bed with someone who looked like famous film director! Or better yet, you might wake up surrounded by the remnants of a wild orgy, with hungover naked movie executives just begging you to sign up with them because you are such fun to be around. It's all happened – but not to me. Sadly!

One of my most memorable 'after-press-junket' parties at the hotel took place in rooms 210 and 211. They weren't actually next to each other as you might expect, but were separated by a fire exit, a stairwell and a sort of L-shaped corridor.

It was the last Saturday night of the month, and it seemed that everyone in London had just been paid and was out for a good time, with plenty of cash to splash around. It was busy everywhere, with numerous groups of people completely self-absorbed in their own versions of a good night out. It was absolutely crazy in this part of West London that you would be forgiven for thinking that there must be a full moon and all the demons were out, getting drunk and raising hell.

That night, with the after-party in full swing in rooms 210 and 211, I received a complaint from the guests on the first floor, who were unable to sleep because of the noise coming from the rooms above their ceiling.

"I'm terribly sorry, sir," I said. "I will investigate immediately."

I took the lift up to the second floor, and as soon as the lift doors opened, I could hear the thumping bass of music turned up loud, on top of screaming and shouting coming from the end of the corridor. Uh-huh. They weren't exaggerating. That was quite some noise.

As I walked towards the epicentre of the sounds, I couldn't help but notice some incredibly stunning ladies walking out of room 210 and heading around the corner to 211. As I approached 210, I saw that the door was about to swing closed, so I hurriedly wedged my right foot in the gap to stop it, and, leaning my shoulder against the door, I pushed it open. The noise exploded around me – music and talking, groans and cries. As I entered, I was alarmed to see that in the middle of the pitch-dark room, directly on the plush grey wool carpet, a makeshift campfire was blazing away!

What the...?

I took in the scene within a couple of seconds, my mouth hanging open in amazement. Aside from the glow of the fire, there was no light in the room. All the other lights, including the table lamps, were off. As I moved towards the centre of the room, in the orange light of the flickering flames projected through the gloom, I could see that there must have been at least 25 to 30 people in there, just moving black silhouettes in the grey darkness tinged with firelight. A few people were lounging on the sofa, some were seated on the window ledge and there were three couples uninhibitedly indulging in intercourse, all in different positions, on the super king-size bed. As for the rest, there was a lot of loud, animated chatter and laughter, and some pretty wild dancing. On the surface of the desk – or 'study', as we liked to call it – there was a vast amount of white powder, and a lot of the side tables were dusted with it, and scattered in the other detritus of drug-taking – razor blades, twists of cigarette papers, syringes.

"You must be kidding me!" I barked, unable to believe my eyes. "Where the hell do you think you are?"

The thumping music was coming from an iPhone attached to a docking station. I took the phone out of its place, so the music stopped and people stopped short in their chatter, wondering what was happening. In the sudden silence, it was as though everything went into slow motion. Everything except for the group on the bed, who were so absorbed were they in what they were doing that they still thrusted and moaned and groaned. More people came out of the bathroom in a state of disarray.

I immediately took a fire extinguisher to the campfire on the carpet and switched on the main lights in the room. There was a universal cry of disappointment and anger, as people squinted painfully in the sudden glaring light. The damage was clear to see. The place was trashed.

The whole thing really was quite unbelievable. How could anyone think it was all right to behave in such a way? Doing this in the privacy of their own home would be bad enough, but in an almost public place?

"Get out!" I lost it for a moment and couldn't stop shouting: "Get out! GET OUT!"

I stormed out into room 211, yelling and ushering people out of a similarly hellish scene. "Everybody OUT!"

Before I knew it, both rooms were cleared of people, and my sanity started to return. After all, it's easy to see how a party like that, which may have started out innocently, could get out of control, even without the sex and drugs. It was a serious situation, though. No one in either of the rooms had shown any ownership or leadership, or taken any responsibility. No one had admitted, "I booked these rooms."

Luckily, we knew the rooms had been booked through a music company, so tracking down who was going to pay for the mess wasn't going to be a problem. The bloody cheek!

But it was times like this that made me wish I wasn't the manager. Sometimes, I thought it would be a far happier outcome all round if I could just fade into the background and let someone else take over. But that's the hazard of a well-paid job with responsibility, I suppose. Still, you never imagine having to deal with such things when you sign on the dotted line. I didn't, anyway.

In the face of situations developing around the

world, arising from Jihadi and terrorist attacks at leisure venues, you would have thought that all hotels, restaurants and nightclubs would have implemented more stringent security systems as a result. Apparently not. One particular night's incident was a real eye-opener, and it made me realise how loose our security systems were.

It was about **8:40pm** when I received a call from a staff in our restaurant to say that a guest had just left the restaurant without paying for their meal.

"OK," I said. That wasn't too odd, but definitely concerning. These things happen. "Was he a resident? Or had he just come in to dine?"

"He said he was in room 312," Milan went on to say. "I tried find it on Micros [the property management system], but it says the room doesn't exist."

"Hmmm." It wouldn't be the first time someone had tried a scam like this – asking a bill to be charged to the room and giving a random room number. But we had to account for the shortfall, and that wasn't going to help any of us to meet our income targets. And I would have to ensure that I had done all that I could to address the issue, if only to prove it to Dana.

"Could I leave it with you, please?" Milan asked.

"Yes. That's fine. I'll look into it further... Oh, wait – did the guest actually sign their bill?"

Milan said yes, so I asked him, "Can you bring the cheque to the office?"

"Yes, sure," replied Milan.

Within fifteen minutes, Milan had brought the cheque to me, and regardless of the room number being clearly stated, I started to look on our system for the name that was written on it. I was half-expecting to be unable to find anything under that name, but when I looked it up, I realised that the name matched that of a guest who was supposed to have checked out that afternoon. That gave me a glimmer of hope. Maybe he hadn't checked out after all.

Straight away, I called the room to ascertain if the named guest was still in his room. The phone rang out without being answered, so I called the housekeeping department to find out the status of the room.

Maria in Housekeeping said, "Yes. Definitely, the room has been vacated. There is no one there at the moment. It's all been cleared and cleaned."

This was really quite alarming, even though the bill was only £35.87. Not a lot, but I knew that I had to carry out a full investigation, because as a last resort, I needed to write an explanation on the cheque, saying why we had allowed a guest to have a free meal. All other possible solutions should have been explored before that.

I went over to the restaurant and spoke to Milan and the other staff members, asking them to give me a description of the guest.

"He was white, and he had a beard," said Milan. "Dark hair."

"OK. A beard. That helps," I said.

"Mid-twenties, I'd guess," said Anna, the hostess. "Well, mid to late twenties, at a push."

They also told me he was wearing a lime green jumper and brown chino trousers. All this information was useful, because it gave me something to go on. Now I could ask the other staff if they had seen where he went.

I spoke to Nicholas, our concierge, to find out if he had seen anyone matching the same description and he responded quizzically, "Funny you're asking about that guest."

"Why?"

"I just thought it was odd…" I raised my eyebrows, signalling for him to explain. He went on to say, "I saw the same guest on the second floor and then, weirdly enough, on the first floor."

"When?"

"Approximately fifteen minutes ago, while I was delivering guests' luggage on those floors."

"OK," I said warily, waiting for more.

Nicholas said, "I thought he was behaving oddly, because he was walking along aimlessly, and he seemed to be looking at every door as he went by, as if he wasn't heading anywhere in particular. You know – most people set off for their room, or the desk, or wherever, with a sense of purpose and direction. But he was strolling along, not really looking directly where he was going. He didn't even seem to be looking for a specific door number."

"Did you speak to him? Ask if you could help him, if he seemed lost?"

"He didn't look lost. Just as if he was out for a leisurely walk. Just looking at doors, kind of casual, but curious. I greeted him on the first floor, and then again on the second, but on both occasions he didn't make eye contact. He just kept his face averted and nodded without looking at me."

This was starting to become more interesting.

I called our security. "Ben, can you check the CCTV footage from all the cameras, particularly on the first and second floors for me, please? Last hour to two hours or so."

"Sure," said Ben. "Am I looking for anything in particular?"

"See if you can locate a solitary male, bearded – lime jumper, brown trousers. Late twenties or thereabouts.

See if you can make out what he's doing, and if you can pick up what room he might be staying in."

"Yeah. Might take me a few hours, though, to check through all the cameras."

"OK. Soon as you can." It wasn't desperately urgent, but if the guest was still on the premises, we could at least confront him and recoup the money he owed. Although it was all quite strange.

Time went by quickly and about three hours later, Ben called me and said, "I've been watching the footage and identified the male in question. The footage isn't comprehensive, because there are some blind spots in the hallways, but I last saw him on the second floor. To me, his movements look a bit suspicious and his behaviour's a bit odd, so I'm going to carry out checks on that floor to see if I can pin down the room he's staying in."

"Fine, Ben. Keep me posted."

I detached myself from that issue and moved on to other duties. As you might expect, it was another busy night, with scores of celebrities dining in our restaurant and bar, so there was a lot to do, alongside the usual checklist of tasks to work through.

As I sat at my desk, I received a call from Ben. "Paul, I've come across something strange on the second floor."

I frowned. "What do you mean?"

"There's a room that's out of service for repairs – room 312."

"Right." That explained why it hadn't existed on the system when Milan had looked it up earlier, trying to trace the guest.

"But the door has a 'do not disturb' sign on the door-handle," he said. These signs were for guests to indicate that, for example, they were sleeping, so their room should not be entered for cleaning. The key fact is that the signs were for guests' use. *We* certainly didn't put them on the doors – especially not on rooms that were out of use for maintenance.

Ben went on: "I tried my electronic key, but although it worked and the lock slid, I still couldn't actually open the door, because it seemed as though it was locked from the inside."

"That's not right."

"Paul, could you check how long the room has been out of service?" he asked. "I mean – it still is, isn't it? According to the system. But anyway, I think you should still come to the room."

I agreed. Since Ben had managed to partly open the door, if a safety latch was still engaged, this meant that someone was inside.

"Sure. I'll check the room status, and be right over.

I'll be there in a few seconds."

I was standing upright again almost as soon as my bottom had touched my office chair. Checking the property management system, it was clear that this room had been under repair for the past six days. But that wasn't to say that it was still out of operation. One likely scenario was that the repairs might have been completed by then, but the status hadn't been updated on the system.

I rushed out of the office and headed for the elevators to meet Ben on the second floor. As I entered the lift, I caught sight of my reflection in the mirrored wall. My eyes were wide and staring blankly as I considered all the possibilities that might be awaiting us in the room.

Before I got out of the lift, my phone rang. It was Ben, the security, again. "I got into the room, and there's a guy in there," he said, in a voice of panic. "He doesn't want to say who he is."

"Jeez," I said, gritting my teeth.

Room 312 was at the end of a fairly long L-shaped corridor that swung around like a boomerang. At a pace that saw me almost running, I got to the door just in time to see Ben using his body to block a man from exiting the room.

"Hey!" Ben said, squaring up to him. The man was

grunting, trying to wrench Ben out of the way and get past. But Ben was a pretty big guy – that was practically an essential requirement in the job description for a security officer. He wasn't giving way, so they were wrestling in the doorway. At first, it looked like one of those playground fights that you see at primary school.

I approached, calling, "Ben! I'm here!" and as soon as the man saw that the reinforcements had arrived, he leapt backwards into the room, followed by Ben, then by me. The sound of the door as it slammed created reverberations, shaking the walls. Now all three of us were inside the room, each looking at the others, wondering what was going to happen next.

"Who the fuck are you?" I shouted. "What are you doing in here?"

"That's what I was asking him," Ben said, glaring at the stranger. "But he's saying jack shit."

I walked over to the man, who was now standing defensively in one corner of the room, like a trapped animal, his hands held open and upwards in appeasement – or in readiness for some kind of ninja move.

"Be careful!" shouted Ben. "You don't know what he has in his pockets."

The man shook his head, his eyes bulging wildly at

us, alert, highly energised. It was hard to know if he was scared, dangerous, a criminal or mentally ill.

"Who are you? How long have you been here?" He said nothing. "I know you speak English."

I asked him in several different ways, using a variety of approaches. I tried anger; I tried conciliation; I tried empathy. "Look mate – I just want to know your name, and how come you're here."

After persistent questioning, all the man had said to us was "You can't keep me here! I want to leave!"

By then I was getting really annoyed with him. I started to look around the room to see if there was any information about him lying around or clues as to how long he might have been inside the room. Meanwhile, Ben stood with his legs firmly astride, his arms open, ready to stop him if he made a run for it.

I proceeded with my investigation. If he wouldn't speak, the evidence would speak for him. The first place I tried was the bin, and I dived my hand into it, using my pen to poke around and move the items of rubbish, like a forensics detective. There were enough food wrappers in there to indicate that he must have been in the room for at least three days. There were newspapers and other guest invoices lying around which, at a first glance at the dates, were two to three days old. The bedclothes, bathroom and towels were well-used. He had obviously been freeloading here for a number of days. That made me really annoyed, so I started to shout at him. "What the hell do you think you're doing?"

But he still didn't budge and he still gave no answer.

"Right. I'm calling the police." I pulled out my deck phone and dialled, keeping my eye on him in the corner of the room. He just stared, broodingly, his body braced for action.

"Hello, I'm calling from the Mannequin Hotel. My name is Paul - can you send someone as soon as possible? We have an intruder and thief – right here. Now."

As I was speaking to the police, the man took his opportunity, and dashed towards me.

"Whoa!" I cried, the phone spinning out of my hand. The guy's speed and power as he barged through literally knocked me off my feet, but thankfully, I had a soft landing on the bed, where I sprawled on my back like a not-very-ninja turtle.

Ben lunged forward and swiftly tackled the man, bringing him down heavily onto the grey carpet and knocking the wind out of him with a loud groan. I scrambled up off the bed and threw myself on him, leaning with all my weight on my hands and pinning down his shoulders while Ben grabbed hold of his arms, wrenching them behind his back. By this time, the room was upside down in disarray and the three of us were dishevelled and from our attempts to gain the upper hand over the man – shirt-tails out, jackets rucked up, a shoe discarded. But we had overpowered him at last and held him down.

"Give us something to tie him up with!" panted Ben.

I glanced around, thinking quickly, and ripped the bedsheet off the untidy bed. "Best I can do. Can we wrap him in this securely?"

Although the guy was still struggling, with some effort and persistence, we managed to use the bedsheet to tie him up in a makeshift strait-jacket, with a tight knot.

"Fuckin' hell," said Ben, wiping the sweat from his brow and straightening his jacket, looking down at our mummified and immobilised criminal.

I regained my composure and reached for the phone again – which had fallen onto the floor. I quickly picked it up. I could still hear the police saying, "Are you still there?"

"Yes," I replied breathlessly. I went through the sequence of events and the police operator said her colleagues were already in the building and should be near our room.

I was still on the phone when I heard a knock on the door and a chorus of voices shouted, "It's the police!" And "Open the door!"

I leaped to the door to let them in. Two officers walked in, carrying Tasers and wearing holstered guns.

"Hello. No need to explain. We've been briefed," one stated, going straight over to the man who was tied up. "Hello? Can you tell us your name?"

The man just stared at them.

"What's your name?" the other officer snapped.

The man didn't respond. The officer knelt down and shouted at the man again. "Your name!"

The first officer moved towards a backpack that was lying at the side of the bed. *Backpack!* There is something that has become chilling about that word in this world of terror and suicide bombings. The officer just grabbed it, unzipped it and emptied it out onto the bed next to the man whilst the other officer continued to question him.

At this point, I started to look at how crazy this situation was. Who was this man? What was he doing in this room? How long had he been inside here? There were so many questions.

While the police continued with their questioning I went on with my own investigation, looking around the room and taking a closer look at the items I'd briefly glanced at before. There were a number of papers, one of which looked like an express checkout bill, the sort that guests would have slipped under their doors during the night because they were making an early start the next day. I soon noticed that there were different names written on at least four bills, with various departure dates. A closer look at the dates on these and the newspapers suggested that the man had been inside the room for at least four days, which, in itself, was truly disturbing.

There were so many things wrong. First, from a hotel standpoint, this room should have been checked by housekeeping staff on a daily basis, just as all the other rooms in the hotel were. So for sure, someone had not been doing their job properly. I was also noticing that the man had managed to get his hands on other guests' express check-out bills, which it seemed that he had used by pretending to be a guest from another room to gain access to other services in the hotel. This was dangerous and a breach of data protection. We had effectively provided people's personal details to someone else without their consent. That is something I will remember whenever I stay at a hotel in future. I will insist that they don't deliver any bills to my room. Otherwise, I might be able to claim compensation or similar from the hotel. I felt the need to look into this with someone from the legal profession.

The man didn't say anything else. But by this time, the police had enough information for them to be concerned as well. One of the officers said to me, "Sorry, mate, are you the manager?"

"Yes, I am."

He sighed. "We know who he is. We were briefed about this chap a few days ago." I raised my eyebrows. "He is wanted for an incident at London Heathrow airport."

My heart sank. What? An airport incident?

He continued, "I'm afraid I can't go into too much detail, but we have to arrest him and take him to the station."

"What the hell?" I exclaimed.

I don't know about Ben, the security man, but it felt as if my heart had jumped up out of my chest and leapt straight out of my mouth.

One of the officers said, "You guys did a great job." He put the cuffs on the man and they led him away.

You're probably starting to see what I mean about thinking carefully before you take on a seemingly amazing job. There is so much that you don't know — until you find yourself dealing with it.

The working hours may have been tough and some of the incidents we had to handle even tougher, but it wasn't all about us managers tending to all the guests' needs. There was some downtime too – although admittedly, not much.

We once had a management dinner at Dana's five-bedroomed house. Even from the outside, Dana Walsh's place was impressive – a stunning white-stuccoed Georgian building in a tree-lined avenue, with its own landscaped back garden, off-street parking and garage. Ornate railings with a high iron gate surrounded it all. What the hell was her salary, I wondered? It was a veritable mansion. Maybe it paid to be a bitch, after all.

I rang the front doorbell, and one of my colleagues, Andy, a restaurant manager, opened the door, a glass of champagne in his hand.

"Hi there, Paul!" he said gaily. "Come on in. Everyone's in the sitting room, but come and get a drink first."

Inside, the house was even more stunning. Original stained glass entrance doors led into an airy hallway with a Victorian tiled floor. The high ceilings had elaborate cornicing, like an intricately-iced wedding cake. Against this background of original features were tastefully contemporary furnishings and paintings.

"Champers, Paul?" grinned Andy, grabbing a slim glass champagne flute.

"It would be rude not to," I said, as he poured me a glass of bubbly.

"From Witch Walsh's stash," Andy winked.

"Try saying that again after a few more drinks!" I said, laughing.

Dana Walsh's house had all the trappings of luxury, and I couldn't help but gawp open-mouthed in awe as Andy led me out of the kitchen. It even had its own wine cellar. I tried to play sophisticated and take it all in my stride, but I'd never seen anything like it.

In the sitting room, a few people were occupying the plush sofas and chairs, but a lot more were standing or milling around chatting. I was relieved to see Stephanie, whose face lit up when she saw me. As she rose from her chair, I saw she was wearing a very flattering, low-cut, figure-hugging, blue silk dress. Her long blonde hair was down for once, curled into gentle waves and swept over her right shoulder, revealing an expanse of creamy neck and throat on the other side. She looked stunning.

I drew in my breath and gave an involuntary whistle as she approached. "Well, hell*oooo*, Miss Sexy Lady!"

She laughed and gave me a playful push. "You don't scrub up too badly either," she said. She tugged at the lapel of my suit jacket. "Armani? You get paid too much."

"I wish!" I laughed.

Her blue eyes twinkled as she looked into mine. "You smell good, too."

"Do I usually smell bad, then?"

She laughed. "Not at the start of the shift!"

"Oh, cheers! Way to make me feel confident, Steph!"

She chuckled, then lowered her voice to whisper in a husky rasp that gave me butterflies: "I don't think you need your *ego* stroking!"

I raised my eyebrows and she simply turned on her heels and walked off, throwing a smile over her shoulder at me, confident that I was still watching her. I cleared my throat. My god! What was she doing to me?

Stephanie went off to chat to someone else while I went across to Dana to say hello, since she was the hostess. Whether or not she was slightly intoxicated already, she looked honestly pleased to see me.

"Paul!" she smiled, her face elegantly made up, doubtless in expensive cosmetics which were more heavily applied than her usual daywear. She was still a damned attractive woman – on the surface at least.

"Good evening, Dana!" I gave her my most dazzling smile. "You have a beautiful home. Thank you so much for inviting me. It's a privilege…"

"Nonsense," she said, casting her gaze around the room, already bored and seeking the next distraction. "Do help yourself to more drinks. Don't wait on ceremony."

I wandered off and chatted to a couple of other managers. My eyes involuntarily sought out Stephanie, and we acknowledged one another's glances across the room. After a couple of drinks, as Dana ushered us all into dinner, I made a beeline towards Steph and was right beside her as we sat down around the table.

Steph grinned at me as she shook her napkin out over her thighs. "Funny how we put these on our laps. I'm more likely to spill things down my cleavage."

"Mmm…" I said, trying not to stare at her beautiful breasts, now she'd drawn my attention to them. I bit my tongue, resisting the urge to come out with a naff line, like, "Well, if you do spill anything down your cleavage, I'll gladly fish it out for you. With my bare hands."

As if she read my mind, she laughed and turned to pass a bottle of wine to someone else, taking the heat out of our exchange.

The evening turned out to be really good fun, and even the evil Dana Walsh seemed to let her hair down, perhaps more comfortable at home, on her own turf. Or lubricated by fine wine.

Stephanie and I stuck to each other like glue. It was just perfect. We really connected, and it was great spending some quality time with one another outside of work, in a social setting. It was an incredibly welcome change and we enjoyed getting to know one another. It was clear that we liked each other and there was a lot of teasing and flirting – it was almost as if we were pushing each other to see how close we could get to spending the night together. I was acutely aware of her physical presence, as if she was emitting a warming electrical charge. I felt her aura even when we were a foot apart. It was as if we had to get closer. Our shoulders brushed, then we were touching one another at every opportunity – a resting of the hand on the arm, a tap of the shoulder, a grasp of the hand, a squeeze of the knee. A thrilling intimacy under the folds of the crisp white tablecloth, as our fingers entwined, explored...

I can remember Dana changing her outfit several times, and everyone ended up dancing – our illustrious director included. One of the highlights of the night was seeing Dana assume a pole-dancing position, flashing more than she intended. Unless she *did* intend it. We'd all seen the Victoria's Secret G-string. We glanced around at one another. *Did Dana Walsh just do a slutdrop?* Eyebrows were raised and smirks shared all around the room while we wondered if it had been intentional or accidental. Whichever it was, life would never be the same now that we had seen her private area – and I don't mean the wine cellar.

By the time the night was over, the wine cellar had taken a major hit. The evening gradually went into soft focus, blurring the edges. We were all gently numbed, comfortable with one another and open to possibilities, our defences down and our inhibitions lost. Everyone looked far more beautiful to our bleary eyes than when they had arrived, and there was some speculation as to which couples would venture off into one of the bedrooms first.

But it never happened. The music was switched off, and Dana made an announcement. "Right, OK. Well, it's been lovely, but…"

She was kicking us all out because it was getting too late. She hadn't eased up *that* much!

CHAPTER FOUR

It was one busy evening, with over two hundred guests attending various events, ranging from private screenings to corporate dinners, in our events space. People were bustling in and out, our solicitous staff all surface-smart and discreet, geared up to facilitate our guests' every needs.

It was usual for events to finish some time before 3am and for all attending guests to leave the venues at that time. This was always followed by a thorough check of the areas to ensure that no one had been left behind.

I say 'always'. I should say 'usually'. I am not sure

why, even now, but this particular occasion would turn out to be one of those rare evenings when the staff actually didn't carry out the security and routine checks, and things were missed. All our events that night had finished early. There should have been plenty of time for the checks to be conducted. I can't understand why they weren't.

Not long after two in the morning, I received a call from the Events Supervisor, Gil. "Paul? Come quick!" His voice sounded panicky. "Events toilet area, fast as you can!"

"What's wrong?"

"We've found a man on the floor. He's not moving. He might be dead!" Gil spluttered. "Oh my God! What are we going to do? I'm in big trouble!"

As the realisation of what we might be dealing with hit me, and with cold fear creeping down my spine, I stood up with such speed that my swivel chair overturned behind me. Without stopping to pick it up, I burst through the door leading into the lobby and ran towards the stairwell that led to the events space. I was there within seconds, panting with the exertion. Gil was pacing the floor, holding his head in despair.

"Where is the man, Gil?" I yelled, my eyes bulging. "Bloody hell!"

Gil pointed quaveringly towards the events space's

male toilets. The doors were already held open with door stops, so I was able to rush in unhindered. As I entered, I saw a man lying on his side on the grey marble tiles, his head in a pool of blood, stained brownish at the edges. It was clear that whatever had happened had been sudden, and had occurred in the cubicle while he'd been sitting on the toilet, since his trousers were still rumpled around his ankles with his underwear in full view. Although the blood had dried on the back of his head, he had evidently suffered quite a serious gash to the right side of it. I rushed over to check for signs of life, pressing my fingers to his throat.

"Is he alive?" asked a shivering voice behind me. Gil.

"Yes, but only just," I answered, having found a faint pulse. As I continued with my assessment and applied preliminary first aid, I looked up at Gil and told him, "Call the ambulance."

I had no idea how long the man had been lying there. All the events had finished hours before. How had nobody found him sooner? The place should have been checked after the guests had left. I could feel sweat beading my upper lip, and I licked it away, the salt tang savoury on my dry tongue. *Fuck! Fuck!* It was one of those situations you can't prepare for, and you think you would never need to – how often might you come across such a thing? But when you do, you don't quite know how to deal with it. I carried on doing what I could with my basic knowledge of first aid.

Gil came back, wringing his hands, telling me: "The ambulance should arrive in a few minutes." Then he stood uselessly nearby, with his fingers in his mouth, biting the skin around his nails nervously. But within what seemed like seconds, the paramedics were standing over me. I can't tell you how relieved I was to see them. Explaining how the man had been found, I handed over to them.

The paramedics got to work swiftly, and before I knew it our unconscious guest was on a stretcher, heading towards the lift that would take them to the lobby and into the ambulance waiting on the hotel forecourt. The immediate emergency dealt with, as the paramedics and injured man left, I had to put on my manager's head and turn my mind to the consequences for Gil and some of the other staff whose duty it was to ensure that situations like this never happened. Or at least, that they would be picked up sooner if they did happen. Consequently, I spun round on Gil and glared at him.

"Who did the final checks after the events?" I snapped. "Where is the log?"

Gil and the others shifted uneasily, averting their gazes downwards. No one had checked. Clearly.

"Do you realise how serious this is?" I cried. "That man could have died! This is why we have procedures!"

I had to debrief them on the incident and the implications of their actions – or rather, lack of actions – finally explaining: "You do realise that a situation like this could lead to you losing your jobs?"

Gil looked shiftily up at me, shamefaced, while the others stared conscientiously at the floor, hugging themselves or twiddling their fingers anxiously.

On this occasion, though, I was lenient. It was clear how shocked they all were. They were obviously feeling a great deal of guilt about the affair, and feared the possible consequences of their failure to follow procedures as they should have done.

"You are all extremely lucky that I am, on this occasion, merely warning you," I said, seriously surveying each of them in turn. No one made eye contact. "Let this be a lesson to you. Should anything like this ever happen again, then trust me – you will be straight out on your ears."

Having said my piece, I went back to the office to write up an incident report. I had started to compose it in my head already. I would be making no mention of the staff's negligence. Instead, I would be stating that their vigilance had enabled a positive outcome to come out of what was a potentially fatal event.

I checked my watch. It was just after 2.40 am. Phew! I just needed a five-minute break, to regain my composure. I picked up the swivel chair I had pushed over when I'd hurried out of the office. But before I could even sit down, my phone rang.

"Fuck it!" I shouted. "Not even five minutes!"

I allowed the phone to continue to ring out while I reached for a drink of water, which I swigged back thirstily. I must have just lost a pint in sweat, through the stress of the incident. The phone continued to ring and eventually, I picked it up. "Yes?"

The switchboard operator grumbled, "I've been trying to get hold of you for ten minutes!"

"And?" I snapped angrily.

"I've had Salah on the phone," the operator went on. "He says they're on their way and they'll arrive in twenty minutes or so."

"Great. Thanks. Just what I need," I replied, and hung up.

Salah was the personal assistant to a Saudi prince who frequently used our private screening room to entertain his very young gay companions when he was in the UK. I'm sure you'd love to know who this prince was, but since I don't want to be hiding underneath a rock for the rest of my days in fear of my life, I'm sworn to secrecy. All I will say is that he has met the Queen on several occasions. He is real. If you don't believe me, just ask Salah.

On this particular occasion, I did have a problem with the situation. It was bad enough that we'd just had a serious incident without someone else turning up practically unannounced. But it was also simply too late for the Prince and his entourage to come for a private screening. Nothing was prepared and nothing had been arranged. It was just ridiculous that someone would spontaneously demand to host a private event at 3am. But at the same time, he wasn't someone you could just say 'no' to – and there were so very many reasons why I couldn't say no to the Prince. Basically, I had to do it, or look for another job.

Gil and his staff had finished clearing up and had locked the events area. Normally, their job would now be done. But on account of the earlier incident, I had some leverage over the staff, so I asked two of them to stay behind and help with serving the Prince and his guests.

I rushed to the projection room behind screening room two, and within ten minutes I had managed to get the projector and all the equipment ready. By the time I had left the projection room and come into the seating area, with its funky red chairs and blue and black seating, the Prince and his entourage had arrived, and they entered the room, shrieking with laughter and chatter.

Salah headed straight for me and started to brief me on their plans for the evening. "We will need to place a food order," he began.

"Yes, that's fine," I said calmly. "I'll sort that out straight away."

"And it will have to be fast. We are not staying long. We have another engagement to attend elsewhere."

"Very well."

Whilst Salah and I were talking, over his shoulder I could see the Prince with five fairly young, effeminate boys crowding around him, all fresh and recently-blossoming consorts, ripening fruit just ready to be picked. They all had different personalities – you could tell, even from a distance. Two of them were gushing and flamboyant; another was cool and seductive; one was grinning and laughing effusively; one was staring moodily through hooded eyelids. But each one was vying for his attention, as if to say, "Pick me! Pick me!"

Before I dimmed the lights to a twinkling starlight, they had ordered burgers, sandwiches, fries, pizzas and fizzy drinks from the menu, and then I started the film running. I left them to their own devices in the darkness.

Outside the screening room, the Prince's security guards and others in the entourage had ordered the same food, but in addition, they wanted a few glasses of wine and some beers, which they asked if they could pay for themselves, so as not to get into trouble with their strict Muslim employer. Then they asked, "Hey! And can you organise a couple of girls for us, too?"

Oh what fun! I thought to myself, past caring. *Do whatever you want. Just as long as you don't steal the artworks or stain the lovely cowhide leather seats!*

Not that I was actually bothered by anything that was going on. I explained that my private fee to keep my mouth shut was a lot more than I wish to say - cash in hand. On that basis, my attitude was that they could stay as long as they liked.

Salah and I left the screening room through the back door, to find some privacy to conduct our confidential business dealings. As we entered the corridor that led to the events lobby, I could hear the crunching rustle of that sweet-smelling paper with the Queen's portrait on the front as Salah extracted my fee from between the folds of his robe. Without making eye contact with me, Salah reached out to shake hands, as if in farewell. I accepted his gesture and in a well-practised sleight of hand, I discreetly removed the tightly folded wad of money he'd concealed in his palm. You could never be too cautious. There were so many cameras in the hotel, and you never knew which angles they covered or what footage they might pick up.

I pocketed the cash like a magician and Salah and I bade farewell until next time. Hopefully, next time would be tomorrow night. And hopefully, a bit earlier than three in the morning!

As I walked through the events corridor and past the distinctive studio lamp, shaped like a stylised eyeball, my stride took on a jaunty pace, boosted by my night's earnings. I pushed through the doors leading to the back of house and staff canteen, keen to find a private spot where I could check exactly how much money my handshake with Salah had netted me.

Not wanting to be disturbed, I ducked into the boiler room. But stepping through the boiler room door, I was instantly aware of a distinctive stench and a clammy, viscous liquid lapping around my ankles.

"SHIT!" I yelled.

As indeed it was.

The sensor lights came on, illuminating a flood of sewage gushing out of the hotel's system. I danced like a dressage horse – instinctively lifting each of my feet up out of the mire, then – since I realised it was too late to worry – dipping them straight back in it. It didn't take me long to know that my shoes and other clothing below the knee were ruined by stinking sewage.

"Just my luck, today," I sighed, wondering what could possibly top this, after the rest of the night's events. I would have to do something, anyway. The stench of urine and faeces was overpowering. The switches on the pumps must have shorted out. I could see the red light on the control panel, blinking an SOS, across the other side of the boiler room.

The control panel for the sewage pumps was just up ahead, but getting to it required great courage. I dragged my feet steadily through the thick, foetid water and used toilet roll that clung to my legs. I breathed through my mouth, trying desperately not to splash myself with sewage and attempting to avoid the used tampon bobbing along close to my trouser leg. Gagging, I continued to wade through the cloudy brown water, knowing that if I didn't restart the pumps, the problem would only get worse.

As I finally managed to flipped the switches, I heard the pumps juddering into action. The smell was unbearable and I had ruined both my suit and my shoes. I would need a thorough dousing in something antibacterial myself, followed by a long soak in a sweet-smelling bath to feel clean again. If I ever could. I shuddered at the thought, and tried not to dwell on the sinister brown lump that had just floated past my shin. At least the thought of the wad of cash I'd just received from Salah went a long way to making the situation seem not all that bad, after all.

By the time I'd dealt with the sewage pumps, it was 4:30am. Not much time to sort everything out, complete my normal tasks and get ready for the daily morning meeting. I got out of the boiler room as fast as I could and trudged wetly down the corridor. My mind was playing tricks on me, imagining the horrors squashed between my toes, and I went straight to the housekeeping office to find some clean, dry clothes. Flicking through the staff uniforms hanging on the dry-cleaning rails, I took a suit that apparently matched my size, then quickly showered, changed and ran to the back office. Whether the smell of raw sewage was ingrained in my nostrils or not I don't know, but I could still smell it. I still felt unclean. I should have rung a bell, like a leper, warning people to keep their distance.

It must have taken me longer to get ready than I thought, because when I reached my office, Les, the concierge, informed me that Salah and the Prince's entourage had gone. True to Salah's word, the party had been a short one.

"Can you smell me?" I asked Les, still disgusted. He looked at me oddly and shook his head. I explained what I had been doing and how awful it had been.

"You shouldn't have had to do that yourself. You could have called me – or one of the other staff," Les said, supportively.

"No. I literally put my foot in it," I explained to him. "I needed to react quickly to prevent the situation from getting worse."

"That suit you've got on isn't quite the right fit." He pointed to the hems of my trousers, which were exposing my ankles, and his eyes drifted up to the jacket's sleeves, ending two inches above my wrist. "You might want to think about changing."

Thankfully, if that was the worst of my problems, at least he didn't think I smelled like sewage.

"Since when did you become a fashion expert?" I asked, giving him a sidelong look.

"I'm gay," Les said. "Good taste is an in-built design feature. Also, while you were away from the desk, John Legend had a lady visitor. She didn't know the number of his room."

We exchanged knowing nods. Having to ask for a room number is usually the sign of someone being a hopeful fan, a friend of a friend, or more often than not, a special visitor.

"You should have seen her, Paul – absolutely amazing-looking, she was, squeezed into this tight, skimpy green dress. If she'd bent down, I swear you could have seen her tonsils."

As he was speaking, I heard the lift doors opening and as luck would have it, the lady in question stepped out and walked towards us. To say that she was stunning would have been the understatement of the year. She was a like a real-life Barbie doll, but in an adults-only, very sexy way. I had always thought Stephanie was gorgeous, but if Stephanie was a nine out of ten, this girl was a ten – maybe even eleven.

"Hi, guys!" she greeted us, and stopped to chat. She was American and lived in Knightsbridge – that's all I gathered from what she said to us, because my ears weren't working properly. Blood was rushing through them and I just couldn't stop staring at her mind-boggling cleavage and equally amazing posterior. The sky-high hem of her clinging dress teased at the edges of her lacy white underwear. Some people might have thought her outfit tasteless, but I would have to disagree. On the contrary, it was very tasty indeed, and I could just imagine myself slowly peeling off that stylish little number from her gorgeous body. With my teeth, possibly.

After speaking to us for a few minutes in a language that might have been Swahili for all the notice we took, she gave us a winning smile before she sashayed off. Our eyes were fixed firmly on her ridiculously shapely ass.

"Man, I might be gay," Les nodded, still staring into the air after her, "but even I can see that she is HOT!"

I returned to the office, where I had a lot of report-writing to do to explain what had happened overnight. Despite what Les the concierge said, I could still smell the sewage on me and I would have preferred to miss the morning meeting and go home to have a hot, fragrant bath. But I carried on chipping away at my checklist, and before I knew it, it was half past six and the morning staff had started to arrive.

The staff had cleaned up the boiler room and reported that although there was still a whiff of sewage in the staff area, the water had receded to the underground sump.

With the arrival of daylight and the fresh, clean morning staff, I started to feel really uncomfortable in the borrowed clothes I was wearing. Dressed in a spare uniform instead of my own properly tailored suit, I somehow just didn't feel like myself. I decided to leave the hotel as soon as I could. That way, I'd avoid all the questions and embarrassment when Stephanie arrived with the other managers. I knew I had to stick around for the first manager to arrive, but as soon as I'd seen Manuel, the events manager, and hurriedly briefed him on the catalogue of events of the previous night, I left.

What a relief to get out of there! And thankfully, I had four days off to recover.

CHAPTER FIVE

My four days off went quickly, spent catching up with friends and family locally, as well as a few who lived further afield. I also needed a little R&R, and where better to do it than down at the local pub with a few pints? In addition, I definitely needed some retail therapy and the chance to replace my ruined shoes and suit. The wad I'd received from Salah was well spent by the time I'd finished.

While I was off work, Salah was kind enough to remind me via email that they were still in town and that they had visited the hotel again whilst I was away. I laughed as I read on. Apparently, the service they had received in my absence wasn't as good as the quality they normally experienced when I was there, which made me feel all the more positive about returning to work. The future of my secret bonuses was secure!

Throughout the time I was off, my thoughts would frequently wander to Stephanie. Our connection at Dana's dinner party had been so strong that it was now consuming me. I kept finding myself daydreaming about that night and remembering our fingers playing with each other's palms, stroking one another's necks, caressing cheeks... at times, it had felt as though no one else in the room existed and we could have just ripped each other's clothes off, like that insatiable couple in the tea rooms. My mind was full of possibilities and fantasies about what might happen next. So I decided to send her a cheeky email, backed up with a romantic bouquet of flowers sent to work (not her shared home, of course), just to let her know that as far as I was concerned, the game was still on.

On my return to work, the hotel was buzzing, as always, and the restaurant bar was full to capacity, with a few people spilling over into the lobby. Stephanie wasn't working that day, so I had no distraction from work. Except for a delightful chat with Ra-Ra.

If you have ever worked in a hotel at any level, you find that there are always particular guests you are genuinely pleased to see and with whom you enjoy talking. For me, one such person was fashion house owner Rachel Wilson – affectionately known as Ra-Ra – who was my favourite guest of all time. Dark-haired, vivacious, and eminently fashionable, she was intriguing as much for her smartness and success as for being effortlessly gorgeous. She had an amazing wardrobe, and an equally amazing ability to party. When she was enjoying some downtime, her favourite pink cocktail was never too far from her reach.

Rachel is Australian, the great-granddaughter of Ernest Asser, co-founder of classic Jermyn Street shirt-makers Turnbull and Asser, and it seemed that she had inherited both his sense of style and his business acumen. She is best known as the owner-director of the fashion house Peridot London, which she founded in order to offer the kind of deluxe, tailored, yet chic and trendy clothes she wanted to wear herself, as a successful businesswoman with a busy life. She hated having to dash straight from work to a cocktail party or event wearing her work clothes, so she designed a range of elegant outfits suitable for businesswomen to wear to the office and then take straight on to parties.

Despite her business interests in Australia, her clothing ranges were all made in Britain. "The quality and finish on fabrics is much better in Europe," she said.

We were very glad to host her whenever she was here. Despite owning over two hundred pairs of luxury designer shoes – everything from Jimmy Choo to Prada – she loved to wander around the hotel in the complimentary bathroom slippers that came with her room. Rachel was a friend to most of us at Hotel Mannequin, but I, in particular, felt an almost magnetic connection with her. If I was working when she was staying at the hotel, she and I would walk into the lobby at the same time and instinctively find each other, even if the lobby was crowded and busy. It was almost as though we were linked by a sixth sense. We often shared our intimate thoughts in passing discussion, from our love of the planet Jupiter to Porky the no-legged pussycat. I greatly enjoyed the time she spent with me chatting in the hotel before she dashed off to business meetings or parties.

None of my shifts at the Mannequin Hotel were uneventful. Many nights started off calm and peaceful, only to be interrupted by the ominous ringing of the duty manager's phone – and one particular night was no exception. My first call of the evening was from Mr

Al Khalifa, a regular guest at the hotel. He was very discreet and reserved, so no one knew anything about him, but he must have been very wealthy, since he could easily rack up a bill for £20,000 on top of his accommodation during a ten-day stay. He rarely emerged from his room during the day, so there weren't many opportunities to meet him, which gave him an air of mystery in itself. Unless you saw him when he checked out, your best bet for seeing him at all was after midnight, when he and his entourage of drug-addled transsexuals and transvestites would be leaving for a night on the town. That was quite a sight to see: a self-contained crowd of colourfully-dressed, heavily made-up trans women, gay men and drag queens, squawking and shrieking with laughter, like a tornado in high heels. Mr Al Khalifa was the simply-dressed, shy and silent one in the middle of that explosion of flamboyance, with all the rest trying to talk to him at the same time.

Up until then I'd never actually met Mr Al Khalifa, but my opportunity came when reception called to tell me that he had forgotten the PIN number for his bedroom safe. He always liked to stay in one of the junior suites overlooking the back alleys, and on this particular occasion he was in suite number 309. Armed with both override keys and a screwdriver to cover all eventualities, I went up to the suite and rang the doorbell.

He opened the door shiftily and took my hand, saying, "Follow me." Leading me into the room, he gestured towards the safe, adding quietly, "I hope you can open it."

I replied with a smile, "Oh, certainly. I have some gadgets here that should do it. It won't take long."

As I removed the screwdriver and key from my pocket and started the process to override the locked safe, I could feel Mr Al Khalifa staring at me. Then he knelt down beside me. "I don't know you," he said softly, "but this is for you to pretend that you kept your eyes closed whilst you were opening the safe."

He placed a generous quantity of scrunched-up bank notes in my jacket pocket. I was gobsmacked, and more than a little worried about what on earth I was going to see upon opening the safe door. Not knowing quite what to think, or what to expect, I gazed at him blankly.

"OK," I squeaked, as the safe door popped free. As I pulled the small, solid steel door of the safe open and reset the lock, I could clearly see why he had asked me to turn a blind eye. The safe was a mini-pharmacy! A cursory glance revealed a transparent bag full of brownish-grey powder, pills of all shape and sizes, needles and a vast amount of cash. I concealed my amazement with my usual impassive professionalism.

Mr Al Khalifa stood over me and watched as I completed the reset and closed the door on his box of tricks. He said nothing at all, so I simply asked him to set a new PIN number and then discreetly hurried back to my office, keen to put what I'd just seen out of my mind.

Little did I know it, but this was the last time I would see Mr Al Khalifa alive. I'm not sure how the police investigation turned out in the end, but I do know that he was later found dead in his room. He had overdosed.

Before I'd even got back to reception, the duty manager's phone rang again. It was Fran on the front desk. "Just calling to inform you that Puff Daddy – P Diddy, Sean Combs, whatever you want to call him – arrived 15 minutes ago."

We had been expecting Puff Daddy's arrival and I'd been thinking about it while I'd been opening Mr Al Khalifa's safe. But my phone hadn't rung until now. I always enjoyed coming into contact with the celebrities and business people who stayed at the hotel, and Puff Daddy had to be among the most famous. As the manager in charge, I should have been alerted immediately, in order to greet him personally. So my first reaction to the caller was, "Why didn't you call me as soon as he'd turned up?"

"There was no time! It took all the staff, including switchboard, to help get all his luggage up to his suite," Fran exclaimed. "And to deal with the relentless demands of his entourage," she went on. "But the latest request is causing a bit of a problem."

"What is it?"

"P Diddy needs a pair of pyjamas."

"Shit."

You may ask why that was such a problem, but it was pretty clear to me, straight away. Where do you get pyjamas for Mr Diddy (or Daddy, or Combs) at 1:30 in the morning? The man has extremely expensive tastes and Harrods, Selfridges and John Lewis were all closed. I would have to do some seriously quick thinking outside the box. The only 24-hour stores I could come up with were supermarkets. I knew the big branches did sell clothes, but how would our international superstar feel about sporting sleepwear from Asda or Tesco?

"OK, Fran," I told the staff on the front desk, grimly. "I'm on my way."

I wasn't looking forward to pitching Asda or Tesco to P Diddy's representatives, but it seemed they offered the only solution available to us. Still, we would do a quick online search for somewhere more favourable. A 24-hour emergency walk-in designer-wear outlet?

I got to the front desk, where I was greeted by two stunning ladies with spectacular curves wrapped in figure-hugging clothes, who were introduced to me as P Diddy's personal assistants. Yeah, right, I thought to myself. With bodies like that, I could just imagine what they were personally assisting him with.

We swiftly started to trawl the internet for good quality clothes stores that might be open in the middle of the night, but unsurprisingly, nothing turned up. If P Diddy was going to get his pyjamas, it looked like I was going to have to bite the bullet and risk embarrassing both myself and the hotel by suggesting the supermarket option.

"Erm... I know it's not ideal," I told them, "but the only places selling pyjamas that we're likely to find open at this time in the morning are supermarkets. I'm sure we could find a 24-hour Asda – like a Walmart – near here."

"Walmart?" Eyebrows raised in doubt, the PAs exchanged dubious glances and I tried not to cringe. I was fully expecting a torrent of abuse and outrage, but they simply shrugged their well-dressed shoulders.

"Uh, OK. We'll need to go up and talk with P, but...

you got someone who can go pick them up?"

"Definitely," I assured them.

We discussed a plan that might not offend P Diddy too badly. I almost couldn't believe it, but the PAs were happy to go ahead with the idea. After I had checked what size he needed, the PAs left to make their case to P Diddy.

I dashed to the phone to send one of our most reliable taxi drivers, Jesse, on a mission to the nearest Asda with a George clothing outlet within it, to buy a pair of size L men's pyjamas – in silk, if they had them. Silk pyjamas – at Asda?

Jesse didn't waste any time getting to the store in Old Street, roughly 15 minutes away. It wasn't long before we got a call from him, along with a series of photos he texted us. They revealed a painful lack of choice.

"This ain't good, Paul. I don't know what to do! You've got to help me here," Jesse pleaded, evidently panicking with the huge responsibility.

It was hilarious. Each picture he sent was worse than the one before. They were all traditional button-jacketed polyester-mix tartan and striped pyjamas which would be more suitable for your granddad than for an international rapper with a reputation for hip-hop coolness who ran his own fashion design business.

By now the PAs had come back down after speaking to P Diddy. The PA had told him that the hotel would be able to get him some pyjamas from a store called 'George', but she had tactfully 'forgotten' to tell him that George was part of Asda/Walmart. So we were to go ahead with buying the pyjamas by George of Asda.

"P says 'yeah'," reported the PA. "Do what you gotta do."

My stomach dropped. I'd half-hoped he would tell them that he would rather sleep naked. But no. We had no choice but to present P Diddy with our cheap granddad-wear.

From the pictures Jesse sent, we chose the three best pairs – which wasn't saying much – and instructed him to buy them. It wasn't long before Jesse was back at the hotel, pyjamas in hand. Personally, they weren't my style – and I doubt they were P Diddy's, either – but I guess if you have no option, you just have to make do. We repackaged them in tissue paper and a nice box so that they looked as if they came from a more upmarket store, and sent them up, with our fingers crossed.

Fortunately, the PAs were kind enough to take the time to call down to say thanks and let me know that the drama was over. P Diddy's PJ PAs could stand down, and so could we. Momentarily.

What a night! It brought a smile to our faces to think that P Diddy/Sean Combs was wearing pyjamas from Asda. It's just a pity we couldn't get a picture of him wearing them. Well, maybe we could have done, if someone had managed to put a hidden camera inside his room...

Following the P Diddy pyjama drama, I continued with my normal nightly duties, making sure that the hotel's standards were being maintained. But, as usual, it wasn't all peace and quiet – in fact, it ended up being a comedy night all round. Only in this part of London could you get so many weird guests in one place.

I got a call from a guest in room 212. "There's a lot of... um... *noise* coming from the room next door," the gentleman said. "We've got a young child with us, and... um... it's... impossible!" As far as he and his wife were concerned, it was imperative that this noise was stopped.

"Thank you, sir. I will investigate the matter myself, and ensure that we do all we can to resolve this issue."

As I went up to the second floor, I could hear the voices, even from along the corridor. They were both men. "Deeper!" one shouted, gutturally. "Ugh... Ugh!"

"You like it! Tell me you like it!" came the enthusiastic reply.

As I approached the source of this raucous noise, a male in a bathrobe appeared from the next room and stood outside the door to room 212. His brow was furrowed with concern, and he clutched the neck of his robe together in one fist like an outraged neighbour looking over a garden wall. Which I suppose he was. Without the garden wall.

"Oh yes! Oh yes!" came a strident voice from behind the door to room 213. "Give it to me harder!"

"Was it you I spoke to?" the man in the robe whispered.

"Yes," I replied. "I do apologise, sir. I will put a stop to it straight away."

I knocked on the door of the room where the noise was coming from, but there was no answer. I rang the doorbell, too, but there was no response.

"Ah! Ah! AHHH!" The screaming and whatever wild antics were going on in there continued. They were evidently deep in the throes, and oblivious to everything else.

Their next-door neighbour grimaced at me, half-embarrassed. I decided to try telephoning the room from the duty manager's phone, so I dialled and waited for a response. But as I stood outside their door, I could hear the room's phone ringing out inside, being ignored. The man in the robe stood waiting outside in the corridor, his eyes averted, his arms crossed. I kept my finger pressed down on the doorbell, ringing it and the phone simultaneously, to see if I could get a response.

Eventually, there was a furious shout from inside the room: "What? What do you want?"

I stopped ringing the doorbell, but carried on ringing the room phone.

A male finally picked up. "What do you want?" came the angry reply. I could hear it as loudly from behind the door as I could down the phone.

"I am afraid there is too much noise coming from your room," I explained. "You will need to quieten down, since you are disturbing all the neighbouring guests."

"OK!" he bellowed and slammed the phone down.

I stood outside the door with the man from room 212 for a few seconds, our ears straining. But it was quiet at last.

"Thank you," he said softly, and went inside his room.

I went back to the office behind reception to carry on with my tasks. I still kept thinking of Steph. I hadn't seen her for what seemed like a long time. I knew she still had a partner at home, but whenever we had been together, she'd continued to flirt with me. So I definitely thought there was something between us that must be worth pursuing, regardless of her home situation. My own approach was to show that I was interested, although deferential – since she was my boss, after all; and to be, I hoped, romantic. I was playing the long game, because I knew she was worth more than a one-night stand. But again, I also knew just how dangerous it was to mix work with pleasure.

Still, I really appreciated Stephanie and I wanted to please her. We had celebrated achieving our revenue target together; I had bought her some flowers and we had gone out for a drink and a meal, which was very pleasant, but the evening had ended in no more than a lingering look and a peck on the cheek. Every working day, I was careful to be attentive to her, making considerate little gestures. For example, I always made sure she had her morning coffee delivered by room service, and just like a pupil trying to please his teacher, I made sure I left her a red, juicy apple on her desk every day. Perhaps these little gestures were just too subtle. Perhaps it all needed taking up a level – given a bit of 'oomph'. My thoughts now wandered to making things more obvious, by surprising her with a sexy gift from Ann Summers. I could go and choose it after work. Yes! I decided that would be my next step.

I was dreading the morning briefing that day. Everyone was expecting it to be particularly bruising this time, since we'd missed a few key targets and Dana was said to be on the warpath. But it hadn't been a bad night, for once. Far from it. And at least I hadn't had to deal with any old tampons swimming in shit up against my Oliver Sweeney shoes.

The office was buzzing with activity. Steph was in, but I could see that she was under a lot of pressure, dealing with some issue and talking animatedly to one of the staff.

"Hi Steph!" I beamed at her when she sat down at her desk.

"Uh… hi Paul." She greeted me distractedly, diving straight onto her computer and dissecting her emails, seeming to be preoccupied by whatever was in them. I glanced over at her a few times, making it obvious that I was checking her out; then I slipped a folded note just underneath her keyboard that said: 'You look gorgeous!'

I observed that she saw the note but she didn't go for it straight away. She continued to click her mouse, frowning at the screen, as if determined to ignore it. I kept glancing over, eager to catch her response. Then, at last, I saw her hand steal out and unfold it. When she read it, I could see her cheeks blushing pink. I grinned, happy to have made some impression. She cast me the briefest of glances, and gave a wry smile, as if to say, 'Oh, *you!*' But she still looked distracted.

When the morning meeting got started, it became clear that this was going to be another occasion for Dana to belittle all the managers.

"I am extremely disappointed! In ALL of you," she began, her painted lips thin and cruel with barely-suppressed anger. "First, in general, none of you has met our targets. Now, am I speaking Swahili when I tell you that these targets are achievable, and your jobs depend on them? So why are none of you DOING your jobs?" She paused only a second for breath, her outraged glare sweeping across us like a searchlight in a prison camp. "And specifically, Nick, what the hell do you call this?" She thrust a sheaf of papers towards him, and launched into a personal tirade.

We each took a battering in turn as she pointed out all our failings and our inadequacies in fulfilling our duties. It was a completely demoralising experience. We all stood – or sat – and just took it from her, unable to defend ourselves, our heads lowered in defeat and our spirits lower still.

After 12 hours' solid running around doing my best,

keeping upbeat, professional and polite while sorting out all the requests and complaints from guests that night, on top of completing the usual 14-page checklist of tasks, I was annoyed, to say the least. But I kept it all in, as did we all. Afraid to speak out for fear of losing our jobs, we once again allowed this domineering, small-minded woman to destroy our confidence and wellbeing. Seething inside, I couldn't wait to leave, to drown myself in a double whisky: neat, without ice.

I left the office in disgust without saying goodbye to anyone, and made my way up Oxford Street to Ann Summers. I was determined to do something to lift my spirits (and not just the whisky). The one spark of brightness that might alleviate my mood was to indulge in selecting something tasty for the woman of my dreams. It might cheer Steph up too.

As I entered the Ann Summers store, I completely forgot about Dana's ear-bashing. It was like a Santa's grotto for adults – or maybe Satan's grotto. My eyes popped out on stalks, feasting themselves on what was on offer. Some of the shoppers were as eye-catching as the displays. The choice was mind-boggling: naughty books, teasing massage lotion, edible underwear and all kinds of intriguing and amusing toys. I'll admit I was distracted – and spoilt for choice. But after some consideration and a lot of interested browsing and idle fingering, I thought it might be best to go for something that Steph could wear. If not for me, I thought reluctantly, for her partner's benefit.

I ignored the comedy outfits and the crudely pornographic sets of underwear. Steph was a sophisticated lady, and I was looking for something sexy without being crass. My intention was to send her a message to say that I was interested in giving her more than just an apple a day, but I wasn't just out for an easy lay, either. It was a fine line between a clear but subtle seduction and an insultingly lewd proposition, especially since I wasn't fluent in the language of lingerie.

I dithered, peering at the photographs of models in the products. As I ran the material through my fingers to feel the quality, I imagined Steph in them. I was conscious that I might be spending too long sifting through the crotchless panties and poring over the baby-doll nighties. I was hoping nobody thought I was there just for that titillating experience alone, like some dirty old man. I was just grateful I wasn't bald, middle-aged, fat or wearing a dirty raincoat.

The only member of staff to catch my eye smiled encouragingly and came over. "May I be of any assistance?" she asked, her dark eyes twinkling.

"Thank you," I said. "But no. I'm just looking for something for my girlfriend."

"That's what everybody says."

I gave her a sharp look, and she immediately burst into an embarrassed laugh. "No! No... sorry – I am not doubting that!" she exclaimed, frantically waving her hand as if trying to wipe a mistake off an invisible chalkboard. "I mean, that's the trouble with working here," she sighed, sadly, casting me a wry, disappointed look. "All the good-looking guys are taken."

I gave her a tight smile and turned back to the underwear while she sidled away. Trust me to get hit on in Ann Summers!

In the end, I chose a sheer, short black negligee with an uplifting bra top that would really emphasise Steph's cleavage, a matching G-string and two pairs of sexy black patterned stockings. They were tasteful yet teasing, so they would definitely convey the right message and make my intentions clear. I was delighted. I couldn't wait to see Steph's face when she saw them.

I had them gift-wrapped in lovely pink wrapping paper, and beamed from ear to ear as I left the store. If this didn't seal the deal with Steph, then nothing would. We had definitely connected and I knew that the chemistry between us was strong, but she needed some kind of motivation to take the next step – and I was praying that this would be it.

It's surprising how time flies. Here we were, several weeks in after I'd taken the job and the only thing that had remained constant was the fact that I didn't like it one bit. The single bright spot was Stephanie.

Oh, and a couple of the other girls who were keen to bed me! Although Steph was the ultimate prize, I had been getting an increased amount of attention from Lilianna and Maria, both of whom were incredibly attractive. "Hey, Paa- aul," Lilianna would say, leaning in a little too close, pushing her firm breasts against my arm. "Have I got something in my eye?"

The first time she said this, I naively cupped her face and peered down into her big blue eyes while she breathed hot sweet breath against my face, panting gently and slowly licking her lips, making them wet and shiny. Involuntarily, I felt myself heating up with the intimacy, as I stared deeply into the whites of her eyes, searching.

"I can't see anything," I said, swallowing hard as I scrutinised. "There's nothing in your eye, as far as I can see."

"Oh, It's you. I've got my eye on you!" She laughed and I dropped my hands and stepped away, eyebrows raised in amusement and embarrassment.

Lilianna wasn't the only one to tease me. If an olive-skinned hand slunk its way around my waist or shoulder when no one else was around, it was usually Maria. I never failed to jump in alarm, and she would laugh and wink a brown eye at me. "Don't be afraid. It's not so bad, Paul!" She gave me a slow, seductive smile. "And there's more of that available. More of *me*... if you like. I know *I* like!"

The interest both these girls were taking in me had been pretty clear from day one, but they had really started upping their game recently, making it known that they were single and wanted a man who would, in their own words, make them "feel like a woman". There was no mention of wanting a guy who would take care of them, be supportive, or who could cook. They wanted a man for one thing only, and they made it very obvious what that thing was. They had even joined forces, and would tease me together when we were all on the same shift.

"Maria just said to me, 'Fuck you'," Lilianna pouted. "But I don't want her to fuck me. Now, if it was you who said to me, 'Fuck you' – that would be different!"

"If it was you, I would, too," Maria added, nodding meaningfully. "Besides. I told her I fancied some cock… tails." Here she leant right in towards me, and said huskily, staring into my eyes, "Paul, do you fancy a long, slow comfortable screw up against the wall?"

Temptation didn't even begin to describe what I felt at the thought of taking either – or both – of them up on that offer.

So, that was fun. And then, of course, the other advantages to working at the Mannequin were the pay and the extra tips I made from all the guests. There might have been a lot I hated about the job, but the money was always a real motivator. Money made our world go round. Mine, anyway, by and large. I know better now.

I was becoming more and more comfortable with my role and the job I had to do, and I gradually started to take on more responsibility. This meant I was trusted both by management (except for Dana, who trusted no one) and staff, and was able to infiltrate every area. As I delved deep into the operations – into the black market or 'underground' activity of the hotel's workings – I became more and more aware of ways in which the staff were making huge tips and extra money, by fair means or foul.

In some hotels, restaurants and bars, staff are

usually not well paid, very often owners cream off their service charge or gratuity, and, especially with seasonal and transient staff. So to get one over on the company, many staff will make what they can out of bad practices and ruses. Various systems and means of deception were used by unscrupulous staff at the Hotel Mannequin, but there was one in particular that was a classic for anyone able to think outside the box. Blink, and you might miss it.

Recycling bills is common. Any promotions or packages offering "two for one", or Valentine's and New Year specials, were fair game to staff looking to make money on the side. Unlike an à la carte meal, which results in an itemised bill detailing different items, with promotional packages, a set menu or offer is provided for a standard fixed price. A couple dining on a special deal will spend exactly the same amount as the couple on the next table, so their bill is the same.

The fiddle goes like this: during the first transaction, waiting staff would print off more than one copy of the same bill with the promotional items on it, and more than one receipt for payment. They would then pocket the duplicates, ready for the next guests.

"Your bill, sir." They would present one of these

copies to the first paying customer, and give them their receipt after they paid.

With extra copies of bills and receipts burning a hole in their pocket, the staff member is ready and equipped for the next customer who wants to pay for their promotional offer meal or drinks. Businesses that are not aware should be mindful that this could be happening to them. There are several other incredible tricks I have come across. All very shocking – you'd be amazed.

"Will you be paying by cash or card, Madam?"

"Cash, thank you."

No credit card machine receipt required. The next transaction does not actually need to be rung through the till because the duplicate bill from the previous guest is already available in the waiting staff's pocket – and is then presented to the second guest.

"Your bill, Madam."

Upon taking their cash payment, the waiting staff give the guest the duplicate receipt, and then pocket the money in full. That's two meals ordered, eaten and paid for, but only one transaction rung through the till. The remaining payment is a nice little earner, cash in hand. In some of the cases I came across, members of staff would use the same bill for several different guests, and take for themselves whatever cash the guests paid. This could be very lucrative indeed.

As I settled into the job and got to know people, developing better relationships with the staff, I started to explore further. Even more was revealed. You only had to observe closely. Certain staff, those whose trust I had earned, told me outright what was going on.

Another ruse that staff used involved padding out the drinks bills of high-rollers by charging them for extra bottles of expensive wines and champagnes that hadn't actually been ordered or consumed. Few wealthy people took the trouble to scrutinise every item, especially if they were hosting parties and events, so it was easy to charge someone for an odd item, like a bottle of champagne that hadn't actually been bought by them or served. However, as far as the hotel accounts were concerned, that bottle was now paid for. Or 'spare'. And effectively, 'free'. Therefore, when another guest ordered a bottle of wine, staff could re-sell the already paid-for wines to them – and pocket this cash for themselves.

In the case of a major event with hundreds of guests, staff could easily add several cases of wines and champagnes to the bill. No one would keep count during the event or notice that these extra items had been added to the list, but had not been served to guests attending the event. How do employers change this culture? It is merely down to value and reward.

These practices at the Mannequin were no worse than at other places I have worked. The hotel management itself was not averse to depriving staff of service charges or gratuities. In addition to the high cost of their meals, some hotels charge more than 10% as a service charge. This discretionary charge, added to guests' bills on top of the price of their meals and drinks, is meant to be solely for the service provided by waiting staff, as its title suggests. There is a debate to be had about what gratuities or service charges should be used for and how, and who should get the benefit. That is, whether both company and staff should benefit equally.

Slowly but surely, I began to gather more information about what was going on behind the scenes at the hotel. Some of this material was potentially litigious, through a combination of personal information and gossip. In fact, there are many things I dare not divulge, even to this day.

It was not only the celebrities' lives that were scandalous. I acquired a whole expanse of knowledge about the sort of tabloid exploits that were prevalent amongst the staff as well. I learned which staff were cheating on their partners and with whom, and which staff were secretly bisexual. I acquired information about dismissal-worthy goings-on, such as which staff were taking cocaine and who regularly drank alcohol during their shift.

As a manager, although my duty was to the hotel company, I wanted to build trust with the staff. I wanted them to feel comfortable with me so that they would carry on feeding me this information, so I didn't always take immediate action. Knowledge is power. Of course, I kept an eye on the staff who drank, did drugs or were light-fingered, but I only hauled them over the hot coals when it was absolutely appropriate or when the evidence was undeniable.

Otherwise, I kept this information to myself. After all, you never knew when it would come in handy. For writing a book, perhaps.

CHAPTER SIX

I went to work that evening filled with hope that the sexy surprise gift I'd bought for Stephanie would be a game-changer. I couldn't help grinning to myself at the thought of what was smouldering away in my bag. It was burning a hole in it, it was so hot!

When I first arrived in the lobby for that shift, I saw a gentleman having a discussion with Fran at reception. He was evidently trying to check in. As I got closer, I recognised him as the director Steve McQueen. *Wow!* I shouldn't be amazed any more, but it still gave me a small thrill to see famous people in the flesh. My standard approach was never to be obsequious towards them or fan-boy them, but simply to treat them politely, helpfully and respectfully – basically, to treat them just like normal people.

At the reception desk, Fran was treating Steve McQueen like a normal person, too. Too normal. "I need to see a passport, please," she told him, "or something of that nature, with your name and photo on it."

Fran is asking Steve McQueen for ID! Oh my God – she doesn't recognise him! Steve had stayed at our hotel many times before.

Before things got even more awkward, I rushed over to intervene. "I'm terribly sorry, Mr McQueen," I explained, trying to smooth things over and facilitate his check-in. "That's fine. ID won't be necessary."

Once he was escorted off to his room, I turned to Fran in disbelief and said to her, shrilly, "Steve McQueen?"

She twisted her lower lip and frowned. "I've heard of the name…"

I rolled my eyes. "Good job I arrived before he said, 'Do you know who I am?' I suppose you'd have rung security, saying: 'Got a strange man here, doesn't know who he is!'"

I left her standing there, both of us shaking our heads slowly in disbelief.

When I entered, the back office seemed much

quieter than when I'd left it that morning, but Agatha, the reservationist, was still busy taking calls and the switchboard operator was similarly occupied. Steph had apparently gone and her desk was clear. *Hmm.* I looked around, scanning the desk and shelves, wondering where to put my surprise gift so that it wasn't obvious to everyone who came into the office. Although, at the same time, I really wanted Steph to see it as soon as she sat down.

And so... I thought, falling upon the perfect solution. *When she comes to sit down, where better to put it than on her seat?*

I quickly pulled out her chair and placed the beautifully-wrapped gift on it. I was just tucking the chair back under her desk when one of the reception staff came in and startled me by calling, "Paul! Stephen Greene is at the desk. Wants to have a word."

Stephen Greene was one of our most popular guests, and he been regularly renting our rooms or events spaces at Hotel Mannequin for many years. He was the CEO of international pro-social media company RockCorps, which produces many large-scale concerts worldwide and encourages people to volunteer through music. He had also been instrumental in raising the hotel's profile with many rich and famous people who had gone on to become regular guests with us. For example, he had introduced many A-list celebrities, including Rihanna, to the hotel. He brought us a great deal of business and had a lot of clout, so as far as we were concerned, whatever he asked for, the answer was always yes.

Slightly flustered after hurriedly half-hiding Steph's gift, I went out to greet Stephen. Tall and handsome, with longish wavy dark hair and blue eyes, he's a genuine, likeable guy with a strong social conscience. Maybe growing up in Portland, Oregon, with its liberal views, its freethinking toleration of everyone, regardless of difference, and its excellent music scene, helped to shape him into the generous businessman, music promoter and community-minded philanthropist that he is now. He has served on the boards of a number of charities and was an advisor for War Child, an organisation that supports children affected by war, such as child soldiers and other young victims of conflict. He's an all-round great guy in humanitarian terms as well as being a successful businessman, and on a personal level he is very likeable, too.

"Paul, my man!" he beamed as soon as he saw me, grasping my hand to shake it, and playfully clapping my upper arm with his other hand.

Like Rachel Wilson, Stephen was a guest with

whom I got on really well, and, as always happened when I hadn't seen him for a while, there was a bit of catching up to do on both sides. He wasn't staying with us that evening – he lives in London, but he often used us as a venue for events and to accommodate his guests and performers. Unlike some prestigious guests we suffered from, he was down-to-earth and always reasonable in his demands. His requests of us were generally not too challenging, and we were usually easily able to accommodate whatever he wanted.

"I'm hoping you can help me," he said, rubbing his hands together and looking boyishly expectant. "Bit short notice, but I know from experience that you can make miracles happen, Paul!"

I smiled. "I try!"

"Have you got a private room available, for entertaining around twenty people or so – business colleagues and friends? Drinks – nibbles – you know the kind of stuff. But really, I need it as soon as you can."

On this particular occasion, Stephen wanted to host an impromptu champagne celebration. The hotel's drawing room was the ideal place, and, better still, it was available.

"Of course. I'll sort it out for you right now. Leave it with me," I told Stephen and headed off to get everything ready.

The drawing room was a beautifully-furnished room, designed to have the appearance of an elegant but homely modern country house. Floor-to-ceiling windows with square panes filled the room with light during the daytime, with columns of cerise and lime broad-striped drapes breaking up the expanse of glass. The soft pink walls gave a warmth and intimacy to the space, and the assortment of coffee tables, rugs, companionable velvet and tartan tub chairs and fabric chesterfields scattered with cushions provided a comfortable informality.

We briskly prepared the room, laying out side-tables with dishes of green olives, assortments of nuts, trays of canapés and ice-buckets of champagne. Whilst I was still inside the room attending to the final touches, Stephen and his colleagues wandered in, ready to help themselves to the drinks and nibbles. I acknowledged his presence and discreetly left them to proceed with his event.

With most events like this, we tended to 'bend' our liquor license rules, if I can put it that way. As a non-resident guest who hadn't pre-booked and was requiring service outside our licensed hours, we had to put him down as a 'resident guest' in order to serve him alcohol and take payment. We often had to do this, since there were many nights when we would receive requests from various celebrities for after-parties or similar events.

One such occasion was the night I had a call from Oasis's Noel Gallagher at one o'clock in the morning, saying, "I wanna bring some mates round for a party."

"Certainly, sir. How many guests?"

He told me it was for fifteen of his friends. No problem, sir.

Fifteen minutes later, around 55 people turned up.

Initially, small groups of three or four people trailed in, and we politely ushered them through to the comfortable, spacious room we had allocated. But the people kept on coming, and most of them had already been partying pretty hard, by the look of them: staggering in and shouting. We couldn't really turn them away – after all, this brought good revenue into our hotel. We just accepted the situation and accommodated them with drinks, food and general service.

The Gallagher brothers were renowned for their wild, brawling drink and drugs-fuelled lifestyle when Oasis were at the height of their Brit-pop fame from the mid-90s, and even afterwards, up to the time when Noel left the band in 2009 after much-publicised infighting with his brother, Liam. When Noel lived at his home in London, Supernova Heights, he once referred to his house as "a continuous party with an open bar". In one interview with *The Guardian*, he spoke of his marriage to Meg Mathews, saying: "We met through drugs. Our relationship was surrounded by drugs. We got married when we were pissed, though we weren't drunk when we decided to get married."

I suppose I should have been grateful that it was Noel Gallagher, who was the one who booked in that night, because in the same newspaper interview, Noel described his brother Liam in no uncertain terms: "If it wasn't for me he'd think it was all right to go on a bender for three days and not see his kid. There's two sides to Liam: when he's pissed he's fuckin' horrible and I hate him, and I really mean that. I fuckin' hate him. It's just psychotic alcohol bullshit and I've got no time for him."

So, with slightly more sensible Noel making the booking, our spontaneous event would have been fine, except for the fact that 'psychotic alcohol bullshitting' Liam was there, too, that night at the Mannequin. And, to say that Noel's party got out of control would be an understatement. The guests were overly drunk and loud, and drugs were being passed around freely. The hotel did not condone this sort of behaviour.

Smoking in the hotel's public rooms was, of course, banned, but still, the heavy smell of marijuana filled the drawing room. People were shouting loudly, music was blaring, and it was all getting a bit out of hand. There weren't any fights, as such, but the overcrowding and alcohol-induced staggering, lack of balance and general careless clumsiness meant that people were lurching about, crashing on top of coffee tables and knocking things over. Some of the furniture in the room got broken, bottles and glasses were smashed on the floor or knocked over, spilling their contents and staining the soft furnishings, and overall, it was loud and dangerous.

I'd witnessed some pretty full-on partying at the hotel in my time, but this was something else. I actually felt quite intimidated, and considered having to take some action on a couple of occasions. I made sure that security was on hand a discreet distance away, but otherwise, we grinned and bore it. Admittedly, it's also pretty cool seeing a hardened rocker and his band partying hard. Although I was risking the wrath of Dana for not taking control of the situation as duty manager, I allowed their hardcore partying to carry on unhindered, in the hope that they would run out of steam within a couple of hours.

How wrong could I have been? The party started

off at about 1.15 am and went on until 9 am, when, running out of steam, energy and drugs, the fun finally trailed off and people gradually filtered out.

At least no fire alarms were set off or people killed. This time. But the scenes of drunken carnage went on and on. By the time the other hotel guests were coming down for breakfast, looking slightly bewildered, there were still high and unhinged party people causing chaos in the lobby. Many of the other guests didn't recognise Noel and his brother at all, so they must have wondered what kind of hotel it was, exactly, that they'd booked into where we would allow random guests to destroy the place with such noise, wild behaviour and breakages. Whereas those who did recognise the Gallaghers asked them for autographs and took selfies!

What a night that was.

Back to the former, on the night of Stephen Greene's small party. After the event was over and the guests had left, I decided to go for a walk around the public areas in the hotel. In the lobby, walking towards the reception desk, I bumped into one of the concierges, Les.

"Just patrolling the perimeter," I said, laughing.

"I might as well join you," he said. "Nothing much happening here."

We took a stroll into the drawing room where Stephen Greene had hosted his party earlier, to find some couples making the most of the now-quiet room.

"Can you smell smoke?" Les asked, wrinkling his nose.

I sniffed but I did not notice anything different about the air quality. "Can't say that I do."

He frowned, then shrugged it off. "Must be me then."

We drifted over to the restaurant and bar, which had only about four patrons in it, since we were about to close those areas. As I walked through the restaurant, I noticed that my eyes had started to water and the room seemed a little hazy. But still, unlike Les, I did not smell any smoke. This was starting to get a little bit weird. But I shrugged it off. Les's mention of smoke must have had some psychosomatic effect on me – making me feel as if my eyes should water and my vision be hazy. I must have been imagining it. Surely?

I acknowledged the security guard, Marc. "Evening!" He jumped to attention, as if he had been slacking or something, which amused me. He immediately moved towards the remaining guests and explained to them, "I'm sorry, but please can I ask you to use the other areas to relax – such as the drawing room and library? The bar and restaurant are closing now and they need to be cleaned."

The guests reluctantly picked up their drinks and bags, ready to move on.

"Sure you can't smell smoke?" Les asked again, sniffing. I pulled a negative face and he shook his head in bewilderment. "Funny, with me being a smoker, they reckon your sense of smell and taste aren't so good. So how come I'm smelling smoke everywhere? Or maybe I'm just hallucinating because I'm obsessed and needing my fix."

"Maybe so," I laughed, my eyes scanning the area as if I might see something suspicious. Like a bonfire. Or not. I took a deep breath and sighed. "Anyway, I'd better go. I need to get back to work."

"I'm going outside." Les winked. "All this talk of smoke – I feel like a cigarette!"

Les and I went off in separate directions, and I was left to my own thoughts. This was all a bit odd, though. Just to double check, before going back to my paperwork, I went off to scrutinise the fire panel – the monitoring display for all the fire sensors in the building. Maybe there was something wrong, since the smoke alarms hadn't gone off. But the sensors looked OK – just the same as they always did. I knew I didn't need to worry unless it was showing the words "general fault" on the main LED display screen. Nope. Nothing. Seeing "general fault" would be enough to convince me that something was wrong, but since it all seemed fine, I shrugged, continued onwards to the back office and carried on with my work.

After I'd spent about 15 minutes in the office writing my responses to the nightly task list, Les came back to see me, in obvious concern. "Paul, you should come and have a look at this." He jerked his head, inviting me to follow him outside the office.

"What's the matter?"

I followed him into the lobby and stopped dead. Now, I could actually see a smoky mist kissing the ceiling lights and forming a layer of hazy fog across the lobby. *Now* I was worried. Les was looking up helplessly.

"That's odd," I muttered. "I don't get it. If there's a fire in the building, the sensors should detect it and the panel should sound the alarm."

"I know," Les replied. "But something's wrong."

"Y... yeah," I stuttered. "Something is definitely wrong."

"Where is it even coming from?"

I immediately called all the departments in the hotel, informing them of the situation and of the fact that we might have to evacuate the building shortly.

"Check your area. See if there's anything on fire," I asked them. But each in turn, they all reported back that everything was fine in their areas.

It was really unnerving. The vague mist was still hanging there, and whether it was psychosomatic or not, I thought I could now faintly smell smoke, too. There was definitely something wrong – presumably with the smoke alarm system. And where there's smoke…

My concern grew. There was only one thing for it – to call the fire brigade. I explained my situation, asking their call dispatcher, "Could you send someone over to check it out?"

Even while I was still on the phone explaining the facts to their control centre, I could hear the siren of the fire appliance nearing the hotel. By the time I hung up, they were outside, so I went straight out to greet them and brief them.

As the fire officers entered the lobby, it was obvious even to them that something was wrong. They stared across at the mist, still hanging in the air.

"Have you got a nightclub in this building?" one of the fire officers asked.

"No," I replied, puzzled. "Why?"

He pointed up at the lights. "The way the light and the smoke are blending, it looks as if someone's set off a smoke machine in the lobby," he explained.

I shook my head. There was no way anything like that had happened. It was a mystery.

"OK. Let's have a good look, then. We'll just get our stuff." And they went back to their vehicle to fetch some equipment.

I gazed up, watching the haze of smoke become even more definite. The more I looked at it, the more obvious it became. The fire officers brought in an infrared machine and a 'sniffer' – a smoke detector – and their team spread out throughout the hotel to search it, in order to identify where the now-huge volume of smoke was coming from. Meanwhile I was breaking out in a sweat, anxiously wondering if I would have to wake up every guest and organise a full-scale evacuation of the premises in the middle of the night. Dana would go berserk.

After ten minutes of checking the public areas, to no avail, the fire officers' attention shifted to the bedrooms. By this time, their radio and communication systems were becoming busier and noisier, crackling with life as each individual communicated their positions and findings. We tried to be discreet, but some guests returning from a boozy night out clearly saw that something was wrong, even though they were inebriated.

"Firemen, firemen, everywhere," drawled one man in skinny jeans, pointing a wavering finger from one officer to another, as his fringe flopped into his eyes. "And nodda drop to drink."

"I like a man in uniform... with a great, big hose," leered a drunken female, giggling behind her hand to her squawking friends. They all screamed with laughter, picking their way across the lobby as if they were walking through a minefield, teetering on their heels and holding one another up. Meanwhile, other guests walking past simply looked either curious or uneasy.

"Just a precaution. Nothing to worry about," I reassured them, smiling. They all thought it wise to go up to their rooms.

By now, the questions I had been asking myself earlier about the fire systems and the reliability of the indicator panel were being asked by everyone – including the fire chief. "Could there be some fault with the system?"

"It looks as if it's still operational," I shrugged awkwardly, since I was beginning to doubt it myself. "It doesn't display any fault, and it's supposed to be fail-safe."

"Hmmm" said the fire chief, raising one eyebrow.

After approximately twenty minutes of

investigations, our first hint about where the smoke or fire was coming from came from a room-service waiter, Lukasz.

"I went up to the suite to deliver an order," he came and told us. "And while I was there, I noticed that the fire was lit."

I frowned. That wasn't right. "But there are no fireplaces up there. Not real ones, anyway."

One distinctive thing about boutique or designer hotels is that there are usually artworks and other odd decorative items put in place around the building, solely for the sake of beautifying the space or adding a quirky touch; simply to intrigue people. Fake displays, fake people – although let's not go there now! This hotel was no different. But such 'interest' items can also be unsafe. Attached to certain walls, for example, we had fake ladders that people would sometimes climb up, and break, and there were four purely decorative fireplaces in the lobby, from which guests reportedly smelt gas all the time, although they weren't even connected to a gas supply. And when guests complained that it was cold, we also regularly received requests for us to light those fireplaces. The fires weren't even operational as open fires, let alone gas – they were purely ornamental. It was a matter of form over function. Superficial image was more important than practicality.

The fakery continued in the bedrooms. Just as in the lobby, in the suites there were several 'pretend' fireplaces that appeared to be real, because the clever designers at our hotel always added real wood and real coal to the fireplace display as decorative features. So the fireplace in the suite was about as functional as a painting, but more realistic.

"I thought it was unusual," Lukasz said. "I've never seen it lit before. And the room was little bit smoky. But the couple didn't seem to mind, because they were on the balcony having a drink…"

"Jeez," I muttered, cursing under my breath. But I suppose you can't blame people. If you had booked a suite with your partner for a special romantic stay at a cost of over one thousand two hundred pounds sterling per night, and it had an inviting open fireplace, piled up with wood and coal – wouldn't you light the fire? Well, that's exactly what the couple staying in the Penthouse had done.

I went up to the penthouse suite with two firemen and knocked on the door, but there was no answer. Whilst I rang the doorbell, one of the firemen was using an infrared thermal-imaging camera to look into the room. "We need to get in here, now!" he shouted, and the other fireman radioed for assistance and braced himself for action.

Hurriedly, I used my override key to get into the room. We burst in and saw that the room was filled with light smoke. The ornamental fireplace was ablaze. The couple were naked and had evidently been asleep on the bed. As we entered, the lady sat bolt upright, giving a strangled scream, while the male shot out of the bed with a cry of alarm, covering his private area modestly with both hands. "What the hell...?"

It was clear that the guests had unwittingly set the fireplace alight, ordered room service, which Lukasz had delivered, had too much to drink, and fallen fast asleep soon afterwards. They had now both been woken up with a shock.

"Get out!" the firemen shouted to the couple, as his colleagues stormed in.

"Wha... what's happening?" the man asked, whimpering. The woman sat in bed with both fists clutching a sheet pulled right up to her alarmed and disbelieving eyes. What had innocently started out as a romantic evening for two had turned into a messy situation involving a crowd of complete strangers in protective clothing storming into their intimate seclusion. Determined firemen in breathing apparatus and heat-protective gear swarmed into the suite with their fire-fighting equipment. The couple gawked, half numbed by alcohol and drowsiness, half amazed and rooted to the spot in fear.

"Please leave this room. You're in danger!" the fire chief reiterated.

"What?" squeaked the female, dropping the sheet, suddenly forgetting modesty.

"So sorry," I reassured the bewildered pair, gesturing with both palms raised in surrender. "Please put your clothes on as quickly as you can. We need to evacuate this room."

Gasping in irritation, but aware that the situation seemed serious, the couple did as they were told and we swiftly got them dressed and out of the room. Having established that the suite next door was vacant and no one else was at immediate risk, the firemen had already begun to tackle the fire, which was more pervasive than had first been apparent. Because the fireplace was fake, there was no chimney flue or proper ventilation, and this had caused the fire to blow inwards, smouldering and charring the wall and causing the ceiling above it to blacken and catch fire. The fire had spread upwards through the ceiling, and had started to take a proper hold in the roof space. The firemen gradually moved further into the room, and the roof space, to put all the fires out.

"Do I need to evacuate the hotel?" I asked, anxiously.

"Not so far," the fire chief said. "Looks like it's well-contained. We'll minimise the upheaval, at this stage."

I breathed a sigh of relief. This was bad enough, without me having to send our entire guest list out into the street in their sleepwear and bathrobes. I shuddered at the thought of the media attention – and Dana's response.

While they regained their composure, I escorted the couple to the lounge on the ground floor. They clung to one another on the way and were silent with shock. All I could do was to find them another room for the rest of the night, and then wait for the directors to arrive in the morning.

Staff walked around like startled rabbits. It was really frightening for everyone. And it had raised a lot of unanswered questions about our fire systems, as well as our sense of design.

The fire service had quickly assessed the situation and identified the problems that had caused this situation – apart from the deceptive ornamental fireplace, of course. Straight away, as soon as they had entered the suite, the fire officers had noticed that something wasn't right. Ordinarily, they would have expected a fire to take hold and blaze away where it was – not to simply char its immediately surroundings slightly, making very little smoke inside the room, and then travel straight up through the ceiling. The fire service had used a special camera and other equipment to analyse the evidence, identifying the issues, and they had soon established that there was no ventilation in the room. This was a concern in itself, even without a fire.

We also hadn't been able to understand why the smoke had first appeared all the way downstairs in the lobby, several floors below the source of the fire – and nowhere else. So the couple in the penthouse suite itself, where the fire actually was, were blissfully unaware. And so was everyone else in the hotel – except for Les with his super-sensory smoke detecting powers, and me with my hazy vision!

After the fire service had conducted further investigations we found that the fire had entered the hotel ventilation system and air conditioning unit, which had caused the smoke to filter down through the ventilation shaft and into the lobby itself. That explained why the smoke had ended up so far from the site of the fire. This didn't give us all the solutions to the mystery, however. The fire chief also needed answers from me. He snapped: "Why didn't your alarm and sensors work?"

"I'm sorry, I simply do not know," I admitted. This was an explanation I just couldn't provide. I needed the engineering team to investigate what had gone wrong with the system.

The fire officer weighed me up doubtfully, obviously finding me wanting. "You must have hundreds of guests here," he said, sweeping his hand through the air as if to present them all to me. "That's a lot of people at risk. This could have been very serious."

"Yes, I realise that," I said, equally seriously. The last thing I wanted was deaths on my watch, and I certainly wasn't going to take personal responsibility for the hotel's failings, but I would be eminently professional in the face of criticism. "Believe me, we will be taking immediate steps to investigate and to ensure that this never happens again."

"Yes. See that you do!" the fire chief said, warily. I didn't blame him. What kind of upmarket hotel puts hundreds of lives at risk in such a way?

We would have to brief the hotel management, of course. This I was dreading – but at the end of the day, it was their responsibility, overall. I knew that my own management of the situation wasn't at fault. I had responded appropriately, as far as I was able. The most serious issues were for senior management to resolve, so that this never occurred again.

On the face of it, the couple might have been to

blame for starting the fire, but so many aspects of the hotel were questionable. For example, we couldn't really say that all the fault lay with the couple, because there was no sign to tell them not to use the fireplace. They were shocked when we told them, because if the fireplace wasn't real, they couldn't understand why that wasn't made abundantly clear.

"Why did you have real wood and coal in it, if it wasn't to be used?" asked the man, sweat breaking out on his brow, exasperated and fearful that we might hold him responsible for the costs of repairs.

"I'm sorry," I said. "It's only meant to be a design feature."

"Hmmm" he said doubtfully. "Well, you definitely need to make things like that clear."

The one thing that *was* clear to me was that if I hadn't taken the initiative to call the fire brigade when I did, there would have been a different outcome. A potentially fatal one.

It was now early morning, and most of the nightclubbers were returning to the hotel. As the fire brigade were all tramping out of the hotel and clambering back into their vehicle. That smoky night shift continued into early morning and while I went on with my normal duties, I still felt somewhat unsettled by the events of the night. I was also concerned about having to report the incident and its implications at the management meeting. But I did have one glimmer of hope to help me face the morning ahead, at least. I was still looking forward to seeing the reaction on Stephanie's face when she saw the gift under her desk. So much had happened, it seemed like a week ago since I had placed it there, out of sight to all but her when she came in. I consoled myself by imagining her beautiful face lighting up in delight as she unwrapped the tissue paper inside the box and saw those fine, sheer, slinky black items. Blushing, probably, before she raised the sweetest, sexiest smile in my direction to let me know she understood my intentions... and even, agreed with them. That one thought offered me a tiny bright light to illuminate a small corner of the darkness ahead of me.

I sat hunched over the desk, one of my hands propping my head while I raked my fingers through my hair and painstakingly wrote my report about the fire. My statement was necessarily longer and more detailed than usual. It included witness statements from the staff, as well as all that the fire chief had told us, since this would have to be discussed with Dana and the other managers at the morning briefing. I was dreading the meeting, since I could not predict how it would turn out. I tried to reassure myself that I had conducted myself appropriately, reminding myself that I had done all I could. Whether that would be deemed enough, I didn't know. It remained to be seen.

Before long I had finished my report, and with a heavy sigh, I pushed it across the desk, away from me. I'd had enough of it. In more ways than one, I was happy that the night was coming to an end. I rubbed my eyes, feeling weary, but I sustained myself with the fact that I would soon see Stephanie's cheeky smile when she pulled out the gift from underneath her desk. I swear to you, that was the only thing that kept me going. I could hardly contain my excitement.

Looking at my watch, I realised that I had a few minutes left to run around and do some maintenance, as well as the usual security checks, so I stood up, windmilled my arms to loosen my shoulders and stretch my stiff back, and walked out into the lobby.

Several of the guests checking out that morning had been asking about what had been going on during the night and why the fire brigade had been there. The staff had been briefed not to disclose exactly what had happened, but if the guest insisted, they were told they should call a manager. And that had been me, in most cases.

"I can assure you, madam, it was simply a

precaution," I told one American lady, who was being particularly curious and persistent.

"Yeah, but…" she interrupted. "What actually happened?"

I swept away her queries. "Absolutely nothing to worry about at all. All is well."

Over the lady's elegantly dressed shoulder, across the lobby, I spotted Stephanie going into the back office, and my heart leapt. I could hardly get rid of the guest fast enough to follow Steph. "Now, if you'll excuse me…" I muttered, taking my leave of her. "Thank you."

I walked into the office after Stephanie, trying not to grin too widely. She was standing by the chair, nervously playing with a strand of her blonde hair and staring down at the unopened gift-wrapped box.

She looked up uncertainly as I walked towards her. Seeing my knowing look, she urgently muttered, "I can't accept this from you, whatever it is. You know that, don't you?"

My face dropped. I didn't know what to say, but I blithely scrabbled something together, stuttering, "Well… um… just tell everyone it's from one of your girlfriends."

She flushed red and carefully tucked her chair back under the desk. I understood from the glow in her cheeks that even though Steph didn't yet know what was in the gift box, it would be a game-changer. She was clearly thrilled, if a little afraid, to receive any gift from me at all. The beautifully-wrapped box was enough to animate her. Just wait till she saw what was inside!

She gazed up at me, holding my stare. There was a moment when it felt as if time had been suspended and all movement and sound stopped, and we stood, breathless, in the vacuum of electricity between us. Then, just as suddenly, there was a shift back to reality and neither of us knew what to say, as an awkward tension crept into the atmosphere.

Flustered, but trying to regain control, I cleared my throat and changed the subject: "What a bloody shift I've had, here, Steph. I've just got to tell you this..." and I told her all about the events of the night.

Steph's eyes expressed shock, but I could also see some deeper concern etched on her face. "There was a problem with the fire panel the other day and they had to disable it," she told me, biting her lip. "But it looks like it wasn't reactivated properly."

I frowned, also concerned. If that was the case, this could have been very dangerous indeed. This was a very serious health and safety issue. Negligence, even.

"And how did Dana react?" Steph said. I looked

blankly at her, just a millisecond long enough for her to backtrack a pace, asking with a wary querulousness: "You did ring Dana?"

"Well, no," I said, and Steph visibly recoiled at my answer. I tried to ignore her obvious displeasure and went on, explaining: "It was really late, and we were so busy sorting it – by the time we'd finished, there was no need."

Steph groaned softly and looked down, shaking her head, her fingers fluttering to her throat as she stood there, distractedly. She slowly lifted her gaze to warn me, "This won't go down well in the morning briefing, Paul. Just be prepared – Dana will probably have a go at you."

"I don't see what more I could have done," I said, defensively.

Steph's eyes were full of pity for me, but her tone was definite and direct. "In any case of fire, you should have called Dana, regardless of how late it was."

"It was all under control," I explained. "But… the penthouse suite will need refurbishing."

She shrugged, looking doubtful, then left the office without even opening my gift. Not the response I'd anticipated. At least, not about the present I'd bought for her. My vivid fantasies dissolved in front of my very eyes and disappeared as last night's smoke had done.

I gave a heavy sigh, recognising that I might have to steel myself in readiness to face Dana's wrath when the subject came up during the meeting.

I didn't have to wait that long. A few minutes later, before the meeting even started, a furious Dana came striding into the back office. Her body language alone made me freeze in horror. She was wearing a killer white miniskirt, black suede boots and, as always, a low-cut blouse that teasingly showed off her surgically-enhanced breasts. But I hardly had time to take this all in, because she immediately launched into her attack.

"Paul!" she shouted aggressively, her face like thunder. "What the hell happened last night?"

She was already shaking with repressed rage. I tried to explain, but the words wouldn't even come out. My mouth was suddenly too dry: my tongue stuck to the roof of my mouth and speech choked me. Everyone else in the office stared at me, wide-eyed in shock. They had never seen Dana so angry. And that was really saying something. Anger was her way of life.

Dana's blazing eyes bored into mine. Eventually, I stuttered, "It... it was a f–fire in the penthouse suite... " I swallowed hard, which was not easy to do without any saliva.

"Why wasn't I called?" she snapped.

"It was under control and was resolved without any

injury or any evacuation," I continued, recalling my carefully-worded report, and presenting the positive outcomes whilst trying to control the tremble in my voice that threatened my professionalism. "I am sorry. I didn't know I should call you, since it wasn't…"

"You are incompetent!" Dana barked.

"That's not really fair!" Steph interjected. "Paul is a very good manager…"

But Dana spun round and gave her a withering look. "When I want your opinion, Stephanie, I will ask for it!" she said tightly, her eyes piercing. Steph knew better than to argue with our boss when she was in one of these moods. She pressed her lips together so that no further outbursts could escape, and looked down at the floor. Everyone in the room, except Dana, was finding the floor absolutely fascinating at that moment.

"I've recorded everything in my report," I began, trying to deflect Dana's attention from Steph at the same time as demonstrating my professional competence. While Dana stood glaring at me, I quickly explained what had happened, including the fire chief's discovery about the lack of ventilation and the faulty fire and smoke alarms.

"I checked them myself, and they were not signalling a fault. But clearly, there is something wrong with the system…"

"What rubbish!" Her eyes flashing with anger, Dana then verbally attacked me, basically accusing me of lying about what had happened. It lasted a good five minutes without a pause, before she hurled some exasperated questions. "I don't believe you. Where's the evidence?" she cried. "Did you take some photos?"

"No," I mumbled, bewildered, "but..."

I wasn't allowed to say any more than that before she interrupted me. "You have a duty of care towards all these guests – and you are responsible for everything that goes on here when you're on duty!" She then launched into a tirade of venom and accusations which I couldn't even take in, only pausing for breath to add, "You should have taken pictures!"

"The alarms are not working..."

"There is nothing wrong with the fire alarm system!" she shrieked. *And yet it had failed to sound the alarm – even when smoke had overwhelmed the hotel!*

"I have never come across a duty manager with so little common sense!" she barked. It appeared that I was at fault for everything that had happened. The matter of the non-functioning fire panel did not enter the equation.

Her words became a blur of white noise, most of her rant indistinguishable in my ringing ears, as she barked on and on: "You should have... you must have... you aren't... you are... never..." She ripped into me, over and over. With blood rushing through my head and the burning heat of humiliation, I felt as if I had blacked out, even though I was still upright and conscious. I sat in silence, my ears humming, letting her waves of venom crash over me; gazing blankly into space as if in a trance.

What am I doing in this job, when all I get is grief? I asked myself. *I haven't heard the words 'thank you' since I started. Is the money I get actually worth it, for this kind of abuse?*

The sole subject of the morning briefing was the previous night's event, my incompetence and how incapable I was. It was a machine-gun monologue of negativity and criticism from Dana, through which the other managers sat uncomfortably with their eyes fixed on the floor. We were all excruciatingly embarrassed but afraid to move or speak. It was pure torture for me, despite my attempts to disassociate from it in my head. I felt publicly demeaned and couldn't even bring myself to look up at Stephanie.

"Is that clear?" She stopped. Finally it was over. Breathlessly, Dana called an end to the meeting and stomped out.

The other managers left the room in embarrassed silence, while I gritted my teeth and did what I had to do. I emailed my full report, outlining all that had happened and exactly what the fire chief had said. Like it or not, there were some serious failings in the hotel's design and systems. This wouldn't go down well with the directors, either. But I had to try to salvage some pride out of all of this. I wanted to prove that I *was* competent and professional, in spite of Dana's opinion. I knew I could still hold my head high – and that she had no case against me. She couldn't get rid of me that easily.

If I had known what was coming in the future, I would have resigned then and there. But, being dumb, I decided to stay the course.

On my way home, I tried to block out the unhappy experiences at work by reminiscing about some of the hilarious moments I'd enjoyed at Hotel Mannequin. Trust me, there were plenty. Where should I start?

How about this. I recall an occasion when a male guest was caught having sex with an inflatable doll in the toilet adjacent to our restaurant and bar. It seemed he was so desperate that he couldn't wait for a more convenient time or place. It was lunchtime. Can you understand the mindset of the person who did such an act? And he was a celebrity!

Another entertaining moment was meeting Tom Cruise for the first time. The switchboard received a call from the scientologist actor's personal assistant to say that he would be arriving shortly to attend a private dinner with his buddy, Ben Affleck. It was one of those not-to-be-missed occasions, and all the managers queued up in the lobby as the blacked-out S-class Mercedes arrived at hotel's entrance. A shorter-than-expected male, wearing a grey suit and sporting sunglasses – even though it was dark – alighted from the car. I was more worried about him falling over or bumping into something as he walked to the front door than meeting him. He looked presidential, flanked by three burly security men and a woman whom I could only presume was his aide.

He entered the lobby and in a deep untamed voice he said, "Hi, I am Tom Cruise". *Yes, we already know that!* I mimed to myself. He walked along the queue of managers, shaking our hands. His grip was firm and a lot stronger than I had expected. I guess he was still in his *Mission Impossible* persona.

There seemed to be a conspiracy that celebrities should be short. I recall the day Kanye West arrived to dine at our restaurant. He didn't have a reservation, so the hostess was just about to turn him away. This was another occasion when I was shocked that the staff didn't recognise a celebrity. Anyway, unlike the picture they paint of Mr West, he does smile.

I was dumbfounded when after he had had dinner, he left the restaurant and went to his car. He came back and thanked me for getting him a space in the restaurant. That appreciation for such a small act made my day. Nowadays, whenever I go running, I tend to add a song or two of his to my workout playlist. You should too.

Another chucklesome memory is of the day Nicole Kidman came for a press interview. Her blue dress is still etched in my memory. During the interview, which seemed to take forever, she asked where the toilets were and someone directed her to our female staff toilets. Can you imagine the delight and the confusion of the girls when the famous actress barged into their changing room squealing, "Where is the toilet?"

I can also imagine how disconcerting it was for Ms Kidman when she saw the appearance of the toilets in such a posh establishment, not knowing they were for the staff. It was our private joke for weeks. Obviously we shared our chuckles with Stephanie, but not with other managers. They wouldn't have seen the funny side of that at all.

Memories like these certainly lifted my spirits, if only for a short time.

CHAPTER SEVEN

I arrived home feeling flat and confused, and with a dull emptiness inside me. I had to cling on to the belief that I had behaved appropriately. I had followed procedures. I was a professional. I had integrity. But these facts, and my very foundations, had been shaken by Dana's outburst and her low opinion of me. I been made to look like an idiot in front of all the managers, which was extremely humiliating, especially since Steph had witnessed it all. I was sure I wouldn't have any chance with her now. I felt emasculated. Although I was trying my best to brush it off because, deep down, I knew I was competent, every time I thought of that meeting, my face burned.

The night had been horrendously long, and what I needed most of all was to heal my wounds by drowning them in whisky. If I didn't deaden my whirling thoughts, I knew I wouldn't sleep at all. So, as soon as I got home, I drank as much as I possibly could, and then went to bed.

The alarm went off six hours later. I had to endure another shift, but nevertheless, I actually felt a lot better. I had behaved impeccably, and my honour and professionalism remained intact. I would show her! I was determined not to let her beat me.

I knew I needed to dress well to feel good and appear confident, so I donned a killer Italian suit and got out a brand new pair of brown Russell & Bromley shoes, slipping them on. I stood in front of the mirror, adjusted my tie, took a step round for a side view, and nodded in approval at my reflection. *Sharp!* Just knowing that I looked good somehow made me feel much better, too.

I glanced at my watch as I left the house. By now, all the senior managers would have left the hotel and Steph would be either at home or heading for home. Suddenly, my phone beeped, so I stopped to check it. It was a text from Steph!

What could have happened? She had never texted

me before. I stopped in my tracks.

Opening the message, I couldn't quite believe my eyes. It was a picture of Steph, dressed in the sheer black baby-doll lingerie I'd bought for her, along with the message: "I've something 2 tell u."

My heart started to race. "Can't wait!" I replied. I went back to the photo and zoomed in to the detail, grinning. Whoa! She looked so hot!

That certainly put a spring in my step. I felt really energised going back to work, and to say that my smile had returned was an understatement. My whole body was thrilled, as if it was charged with electricity.

It was another busy journey on the Central Line into London, and then on by foot. Everyone was hurrying onwards, wearing the same old trance-like gaze as me as I walked through the back streets south of Oxford street to the hotel. In my own mind I was reminiscing about my first week in the job, all those weeks before, when there had been a murder outside the staff entrance. Steep learning curve! And the more I thought about it, the more I came to the conclusion that I'd not only grown into my own role but had adopted the 'house style' of the hotel and felt a corporate loyalty to it. I was a credit to them, in fact!

I swerved out of the way of a grim-faced man, about my age, in a designer suit, a bulky leather messenger bag swinging from his shoulders and a sheet of paper in one hand, a mobile phone in the other. His expression looked pained and harrowed as he read the document and muttered into his phone, the weight of the world of work on his shoulders. I was not going to be *that* guy. Despite Dana's negative feelings about me, I knew that I had conducted myself professionally and my reputation would remain intact. I was respected by everyone else I worked with, after all, and I was pleased to notice that my fears and shock over Dana's hysterical reaction early that morning had disappeared. She could go hang, as far as I was concerned. I was blameless, and she could not prove otherwise. In fact, quite the reverse: I had reacted most appropriately and averted disaster.

So I walked into the hotel with my head held high, confidence fully returned.

"Hey, Paul," said Les, the concierge. "Well done last night." He actually shook my hand and looked me sincerely in the eye as he said, "Good job, man."

"Cheers, Les," I said, bemused. At least someone appreciated me. "Mind you, it was your sniffer-dog ability that first alerted us!"

"Ach!" He waved his hand dismissively, as if to say, 'shucks, it was nothing'. "But wait till I tell you... it turns out you were right," he went on. "They confirmed that the fire alarm system really *was* faulty."

I raised my eyebrows. *Take that, Dana!*

Les sighed, shaking his head. "Just think – it would have been far worse if you hadn't acted when you did."

"Thanks." I hoped the rest of the directors would see it that way.

That night wasn't any busier than any other night at the hotel. The Mannequin was fully booked and because we'd lost the use of the penthouse suite owing to the fire overnight, we had to book one of our new guests into a sister property. If that was my first task of the shift that evening, the next was to think about Steph... but silly me! I was doing that every night already.

"Hi Paul," said another of the concierges, Marcel. "Just wanted to say – thanks for acting fast last night. Not everyone would have done that."

I nodded, smiling. "Cheers. Appreciate it, Marcel. Thank you."

In fact several of the junior staff came over and thanked me when they spotted me. That was really refreshing, and I was mildly amazed by their responses. Many of them told me that several of our managers wouldn't have been as proactive as I had been.

"You're a life-saver!" said Ewelina when she came

in. I laughed, but she exclaimed: "Seriously. Imagine how bad it might have been if you hadn't call out the fire brigade when you did. Honestly – a lot of people owe their lives to you."

I glowed inside with all this gratitude. Even though Dana would never acknowledge my worth, I was really heartened to know that the staff appreciated how much I did for everyone.

But I couldn't bask in glory for long. In the meantime, there was still the usual work to be done. That night, we had several events, including another blasted press junket, so several of our bedrooms had been cleared of all their bedroom furniture and accoutrements in order to be used as press interview rooms. When they were finished, we would swiftly have to turn the rooms back into bedrooms before the overnight guests arrived later that night or the next morning. This was back-breaking work, lugging beds and other furniture to and from store-rooms within a quick turnaround time. It had to be done, though – the alternative would be coming face-to-face with tired, irate guests who were longing to check in and screaming to be allowed to settle into their rooms.

Following the usual routine, I rounded up all the available staff and got them to help to set up the rooms. Whilst we were going through the process of collecting furniture and making up beds, my phone rang.

"Just carry on with the next two rooms," I told the staff, peering down at my phone. "I just need to take this."

I could see from the display screen that it was one of the security guards, Marc, who was calling me. When I answered, he stated succinctly, "There's a situation in the bar. You need to come. Some lady is claiming that her handbag has been stolen."

My heart sank. "I'll be right there."

This kind of situation wasn't easy to deal with. As a business, our hotel didn't accept liability for items that were lost or stolen on our property, so it was up to the individuals concerned to report any theft to the police, and for the police to investigate. And most of the time, people don't think about insuring things like handbags, although if you really think about it, it's usually the smaller things that matter most. Whilst the objects contained in bags might seem trivial and worthless in their own right, the access they provide is of great significance. Think about it: mobile phones, bank cards, pay slips, car keys, house keys, driving licences detailing home addresses... all of these leave people vulnerable to further, more serious thefts, of course.

As I went into the restaurant, the hostess, Anna, greeted me at the door with an odd grimace and informed me that the lady claiming that her bag had been stolen was waiting for me at the host desk. Wide-eyed, Anna raised her eyebrows and nodded her head in that direction. "She's um… a little distracted."

I glanced over to the desk to see what she meant before walking over. The woman was looking down, one elbow on the counter, her slightly ruffled hair hanging over her face.

"Good evening, madam. I am the duty manager. I understand you have lost a bag?"

"Oh!" She jerked to life as if I had just woken her up from a deep sleep. As she swung around to greet me, stepping unsteadily backwards, it was apparent that her elbow had been the only thing holding her upright. She slammed one palm down on the desk and gripped the edge tightly with both hands to get her balance again, while I stepped forward to catch her in case she fell.

"Sorry to startle you, madam. Are you all right?"

She turned her swimming pupils towards me, trying to focus. I tried again. "Can you tell me where you have been sitting?" I asked her.

She pointed a finger vaguely into the distance, and it travelled through the air like a conductor's baton describing a very slow movement of music to an invisible orchestra. "Over... there!" she announced, seamlessly ending the statement with a gentle belch.

"And could you describe the bag, please?" I asked.

"Ha-aa-ah. Um. Right... erm... issa... ba-ag... Right?" From her wavering gaze and slurring speech, it was clear that she was far from sober. In fact, there was so much alcohol on her breath that if she had stood too close to a naked flame, she'd have exploded.

"Iss... got... hangles? Hangles... for handssssss..." She held up one hand like a starfish, and twisted it around in the air to demonstrate what she meant by 'hands,' just in case I was in any doubt.

As we continued our conversation, another lady approached. "Jane? What's happened?" she called to the woman as she strode up. "Why are you talking to this man?"

"Whass? Wosh you say?" our lady replied in a shout, despite the fact that her friend was now standing right next to her. She turned to hug the friend theatrically, bumping their heads together, then screeching with laughter. "I ca-aaaaan fine my bag!"

"You mean this one?" the second lady said, dangling the "stolen" handbag in front of Jane, who stared at it in amazement, her mouth open as if she had just witnessed a baffling conjuring trick.

"Oh!" Jane smacked her lips together, trying to compute the meaning of this marvellous sign and wonder. "Yes-s-s!" As realisation dawned on her, she eventually said, slightly sheepishly, "Thish one. Where d'you find it?"

"You left it in the toilet."

Laughing uproariously, the pair of them carried on as if I wasn't there, chatting away amongst themselves. Fine.

"I will leave you ladies, then. Enjoy the rest of your evening," I said politely as I walked away. Great start to the evening, I thought to myself, rolling my eyes.

This shift continued at a steady pace and, as always, we had a high volume of celebrity guests, many of whom were staying under aliases. Rihanna had left our hotel a few days previously, but earlier that day, she had returned; Michael Bublé was staying for a number of nights, as were Jon Hamm and Paddy McGuinness, to name just a few.

Just after 11pm, as the restaurant was closing, leaving only the hotel's vibrant, busy bar as the focal point for our guests' social life, I walked into the office, only to be met by the concierge, Carl.

"We have a BIG problem, Paul!" he said, in concern, opening his arms wide to show just how big the problem was. "It's Mr and Mrs Burroughs."

I raised my eyebrows. 'Mr and Mrs Burroughs' was the pseudonym Jon Hamm and Jennifer Westfeldt were using for their stay in the hotel.

"Why? What's happened?" I asked.

Carl went on: "They came back from dinner at eleven tonight with no key, because Mrs Burroughs' handbag had been stolen whilst they were out for dinner at a restaurant in Mayfair." Carl paused for an intake of breath. "So they asked us to let them into their room, and I took them upstairs. On reaching their room, Ms Westfeldt said, 'Oh, no! Someone has been in our room!' Apparently they have been burgled."

"How is that even possible?" I asked, astonished. "Are they accusing a member of staff?"

"I don't know," Carl replied. "But they asked to speak to a manager straight away. You'd better go up to their suite – as soon as! They're furious!"

Bracing myself to deal with their anger, I hurried up to their suite and knocked at the door. It was opened by Mr Burroughs, played by Jon Hamm, tight-lipped and stern.

"I'm so sorry, sir," I began as he let me in. "Please let me know what's happened."

"Someone's been in here!" he began. "A number of our valuables are missing."

"Both our laptops," added Jennifer Westfeldt, aka Mrs Burroughs. She was obviously agitated and as she spoke, she repeatedly tucked strands of blonde hair nervously behind her ear. They went on to explain to me that a whole list of items had been stolen from their room: an iPad, two Mac laptops, Jennifer's passport and an iPhone.

"The door wasn't even forced," said Hamm, striding to the door to show me the still-intact lock. "They must have had a key."

A chill ran down my spine. This could indicate staff. But then again...

"And I understand that your handbag was stolen earlier this evening, and your bag had your key in it?" I asked.

"Yes," said his companion. "But it seems very weird, doesn't it?"

"We want the police to come in, to carry out an investigation," asserted 'Mr Burroughs'.

"Of course," I said. I couldn't expect anything different. If an incident occurring at the hotel was not attended by a police officer at the time of its reporting, the procedure was that the guest would have to go and report the incident to the police themselves, in person. And as a celebrity, Jon Hamm – under any name – would certainly not be turning up to a local police station in the early hours of the morning to sit in a waiting area with the drunks, the brawlers and the prostitutes just to report a crime and make a statement. Especially not when it could be easily avoided by us calling the police to discreetly attend to the matter at the hotel.

"I'll call the police at once," I reassured them both, "but first, we'll get you moved to a new room."

"No," Hamm interrupted, waving his hand dismissively. "That's fine. We'll stay here."

"Are you sure?" I asked, puzzled. If I had been burgled, I would definitely want to switch rooms – otherwise, I still wouldn't feel safe. Having your place burgled was a violation of privacy. I would want a fresh start.

"Yes," his partner agreed. She cast her eyes around the room, where their clothes and personal belongings were all laid out exactly where they wanted them or tucked away where they had put them. "That would mean too much upheaval."

Everything – except the stolen electrical items – was still settled in place; her perfumes and cosmetics on the dressing table; their clothing all hanging in the wardrobes or neatly folded away in the drawers.

"As you wish," I said, understanding her point, but still somewhat surprised. Nevertheless I reassured them that the digital lock would be reprogrammed, so that anyone in possession of the lost or stolen key would have no chance of getting back into the room.

Once I made the call, the police said they would send someone straight over.

"They're on their way," I reassured the couple. "But we have CCTV cameras in all the corridors and public areas, so I'm sure they will have picked up something that indicates the identity of the thief. I'll just go and make sure we can access the tapes. The police will need to view them, anyway."

"Sure," said Hamm. "I guess you'll send the cops up when they arrive."

While we were waiting for the police to arrive and take statements, I decided I could be better employed sitting in the security office to peruse the video footage we had available. So I left their room and went down to the security office to locate the recent recordings from the relevant cameras on the route.

"Hey, Ben – can we get the videos from the cameras from the lobby, all the way right up to the Burroughs' suite - 418?" I asked the security officer. "The ones in the lifts as well."

I sat down and explained exactly what we wanted, and why, and Ben got to work. "Probably best to start by looking at the recording from the camera focused on the hallway of the suites, where we know the perpetrator was for sure," said Ben, clicking a couple of switches. "There we go. Got a specific timescale in mind?"

"Well, the Burroughs came back just before eleven, so any time before that," I said, settling into my seat and hunching over, peering at the monitor.

"Let's take it from 11pm and work backwards then," Ben said, his eyes trained on the screen before him. He began a fast rewind through the tape from the moment when the Burroughs had arrived back at their room.

"Hang on. There!" cried Ben, stopping the tape and pointing at the monitor. He rewound the recording, just a couple of frames. "There he is!"

I leaned further forward, my eyes straining to see. At the door of the guests' suite, a nondescript dark-haired man dressed in a dark jacket and light trousers was letting himself out of the Burroughs' suite. Because the video was still running on rewind, it looked as if he was letting himself in – walking backwards into the room.

"Anyone you know?" I asked him warily, peering at the screen. If that thief was staff, this was just another complication I didn't want to deal with.

"Hard to tell." Ben ran the recordings back further, until we saw the man entering.

"Doesn't look like any of the staff," I said, frowning, but feeling a flicker of relief. "Pretty good images, though, Ben."

"Yeah. Not bad resolution on these."

Next, from the other cameras' footage, we tracked the man through the corridors, saw him in the lift and crossing the foyer, and then picked him up outside, at the entrance to the hotel.

"Great job, Ben," I said.

"Cheers, Paul. Yeah. Next thing is, I can cue it up all together, in chronological order, for the police."

He got together the video evidence from the different cameras in plenty of time to show the police, and when they had finished taking statements from the Burroughs, one of the officers came to see.

The officer sat down, while Ben showed him the footage and I talked him through it.

"Ben's cued up the videos to sequence the events in the right order, so we have an accurate timeline," I explained. "Go ahead, Ben."

We watched the footage in the correct order.

"That's the male in question," I said, when Ben started the video, tapping on the screen with his forefinger, pointing at one figure.

The thief had arrived at the main entrance of the hotel at 21:14:19, according to the driveway camera. He had in his possession three bags: two stiff paper carrier bags – the sort that designer clothes shops provide – and a third bag that looked like a black holdall.

"Those bags... they're empty, there, are they?" said the officer, his chin propped thoughtfully on his hand.

"I think so," I said. "At the moment. Wait till you see later, though. But the cardboard ones are quite stiff, so if you don't look too closely, you could imagine there's something in them now."

The guy looked fairly innocuous – just like any other guest who had been out shopping. He set the bags down on the floor while he bent down and adjusted his shoelaces.

"Ah, there, you see," the officer said, pointing. "Yeah. The bags are just too light, really. But only when you know."

"He just seems to be biding his time here," explained Ben. "Apparently waiting till a few other people walk into the hotel."

Sure enough (because Ben had already seen it four times, forwards and backwards), the guy glanced up when a group of people walked up to the door, and stood up, grabbing the bags. I felt like I was in a CSI team!

The man entered the building at 21:17, casually walking in like one of the crowd, under the cover of the other guests. Then he stepped into the guest lift, where he appeared to be engaged in a conversation on his phone.

"Then we need to switch cameras," Ben said, clicking on another video switch.

Cross-referenced with the footage from the camera in the lift itself, we saw the man standing there, waiting calmly as the lift rose, taking him on his way up to the fourth floor.

"And then the camera in the hallway on the fourth floor picks him up," said Ben, clicking on another image.

At 21:20:40, he was seen leaving the lift, walking towards guest room 418.

"This is it. Mr Burroughs – Mr Hamm's – room," I said.

The man let himself into the room, and that was where our record of his next actions stopped. Our footage simply showed the closed door.

"Obviously, we don't have security cameras inside our rooms," I explained

The man evidently spent a few minutes inside, because he then left the room at 21:23:49, carrying the same three bags he had arrived with.

"Three minutes!" nodded the police officer, almost impressed.

The man peered inside his bags, as if checking them, before heading off down the corridor.

"See, the bags are obviously much weightier now," I said.

At 21:24:02, the man was then seen entering the guest lift on the fourth floor before pressing the lift button to descend. Arriving in the foyer, once again looking as if he was talking on his mobile phone, the man left through the main entrance of the hotel at 21:25:35.

"Smooth operator," said the police officer viewing the footage. "Ten minutes from front door to back outside again. And he looks cool as a cucumber. This is no opportunist who's just stumbled upon the key."

"That's what troubles me," I said. "Our keys have no hotel name on them to identify them."

The officer shrugged. "Might have followed the guests. Or perhaps the lady had something in her handbag that indicated the hotel name – reservation, bill, or something."

"But there's still nothing that would state the room number," I interrupted, puzzled.

"Still," the officer went on. "The case will be passed onto senior detectives, since this individual seems to be an expert at what he does. Could be linked to other cases, and the individual may even be known to us." He stood up, ready to take his leave of us. "We'll be in touch to get a copy of that CCTV footage. Can you put something together for us?"

"Sure," said Ben. "I'll get onto it right away."

I went up and explained to our guests that in accordance with the Hotel Proprietors Act, guests had to report the theft to their own insurers. "You'll need to give them the police crime number and report if you wish to make a claim."

"Sure," they said. "Thank you."

I left them, still feeling bemused. There were a number of things that troubled me about this theft. I was particularly concerned, because if the key had been stolen along with Mrs Burroughs's bag in the restaurant, I couldn't understand how the burglar knew that the key was from our hotel, especially it had no logo or name on the key.

It was fair enough to think that someone might opportunistically steal a handbag in a restaurant. That would be an end in itself – cash, phone, credit cards – fine. But it was troubling that the person travel some distance to a hotel and to burgle their room. It was odd incident that was shocking. I must admit that the Burroughs were extremely brave. In the end they decided to stay in the same room overnight.

And thinking about it even more, if you were a burglar, why would you take just a Mac, an iPad, a phone and a passport? They're all fairly useless, and completely unappealing to an experienced thief, given that the police can use the inbuilt technology on those devices to trace them. Wouldn't you be more inclined to steal untraceable items, such as clothes, jewellery, money and anything that you could sell on the black-market for a quick buck? All these things had been left openly lying around in the Burroughs's room.

Things just didn't add up. The only question was – why? It just made no sense at all.

That incident kept me busy all night. From the time it was reported up until the police left, fours later, I was busy checking the CCTV and writing up the reports to cover any insurance claim that might follow. And after the fire incident the night before, I was dreading breaking the news of this one at the morning briefing. This place was crazy! Working in hotels, you certainly see a lot of strange things and have to deal with a wide range of odd events – but here at the Mannequin, it seemed to be a relentless rollercoaster of non-stop incidents. It was all way beyond what I'd experienced at any other hotel I'd worked in.

I braced myself for the morning meeting, not needing a warning from Steph to beware of our illustrious leader. In fact I hadn't seen Steph come in that morning – and she wasn't even there for the meeting. I was surprised that she hadn't appeared for work, though – I knew she wasn't on holiday. I hoped she wasn't ill.

Dana started the morning meeting, grim-faced and barking orders and questions as usual. "Your report, Paul?" she said, her tone clipped.

When I explained what had happened with the Burroughs, Dana didn't hold back. She made it clear that she didn't like the way the incident had been handled, nor how the investigation had been carried out.

"What were security doing at the time?" she snapped. She tried to furrow her brow in disapproval, but the Botox wouldn't let her. "Were the staff actually doing their jobs? Why did no one notice the burglar?"

That had to be a trick question. It wasn't as if he had come in wearing a black ski mask, with a sack labelled 'SWAG' over his shoulder and a T-shirt with 'BURGLAR' emblazoned across the chest. How are you supposed to 'notice' a burglar, if he's making a half-decent job of it?

Naturally my own conduct during my interaction

with Mr Burroughs was called into question. I was in the firing line again.

Dana exclaimed, "Mr Burroughs's PA called my office just before this meeting. She said the manager who dealt with them had laughed in their faces and said, "That's brilliant!" when they said they had been robbed."

I was outraged. "I certainly..." I began, but Dana simply talked over me. I was being reprimanded by her again. Severely. And publicly.

"I will not tolerate such disrespect towards guests!" she cried. "I have had to apologise profusely for your behaviour, and this whole sorry affair has damaged both the hotel's reputation and my own!" she spat, going on and on.

I kept my mouth shut, afraid that if I said anything at all, I would immediately regret it. I didn't want to be sacked on the spot. But really, that was it, for me. I knew it was time for me to leave the job. It was just all too much. I didn't seem to be doing anything right. But there again, I was determined that if I went, I would leave on my own terms – not be thrown out on my ear after getting told off like a naughty child. Or dismissed for gross misconduct after totally losing it and ramming a ream of A4 printer paper down Dana's nagging, bitching throat.

When the briefing ended and I'd allowed my simmering rage to die down, my mind strayed to Steph again. I was worried. I thought it was really strange that she had not come into work that day, and she hadn't called or texted to tell anyone that she was sick. I wasn't sure if I should text her. My imagination began to work overtime. I hoped her partner hadn't found out that I had given her that gift.

I took out my phone and glanced at the picture she had sent me the previous evening, a smile playing on my lips. My God, she looked hot in that sheer black baby-doll...

But... back to reality. Stephanie had clearly been upset at the way Dana had treated me the day before, and she had actually spoken up on my behalf when Dana had initially launched into her attack. I appreciated her defending me. However, we all knew it wasn't good for Steph, or for her career in the future, to express her displeasure with the management.

During the days after the robbery, the hotel, of course, kept very quiet about it. Despite this, information had still clearly leaked out from somewhere, because we received several enquiries about it from US media houses and American journalists. But that was the strange thing about it. Who on earth would have told the American media?

Any of our own staff's communications were with contacts in the British press and TV, overall. They would have been the first port of call for stories. Not the Americans. It would take Americans to do that. My suspicions deepened further.

Luckily, it was easy for us to deny that the incident had ever happened: the journalists were all asking about Mr Hamm, so we were able to say, with complete honesty and integrity, that we'd had no guest of that name staying with us at all. The press weren't to know that the couple had booked in under the name Burroughs.

CHAPTER EIGHT

On my way home, I decided to do a little window shopping on Oxford Street. For myself, this time. No more sexy gifts for Stephanie just yet, I thought. I still didn't quite know how she was going to respond to my last one. Or what it was that she wanted to tell me. Although I liked what I'd seen so far!

After idly browsing around a few stores, trying to take my mind off Stephanie – unsuccessfully – I finally went into a café for a sandwich. Whilst I was sitting down at a table in the café eating my lunch, Marc and Chris, two of the security who had been working the night before, walked in. They ordered at the counter and were just walking across to their table when they noticed me, greeting me with smiles, and came over.

"Hi, Paul," said Marc warmly.

"Just the man," Chris commented. "Mind if we join you?"

"No, do. Sit down," I said, moving my discarded napkin aside to make room, and they set down their coffees. "How're you doing?"

"Really sorry about last night," Chris said.

Having just bitten my sandwich, my mouth was full, but I shook my head rapidly and pulled a face, hoping to say 'don't be silly' through the medium of mime and facial expression alone.

"There was no way we would have thought that guy was a burglar," Marc said. "He looked just like any of our guests."

"Yeah, I know," I sighed, wiping my mouth on my napkin. "Don't worry about it."

"You know what else?" Chris glanced around, leaning forward and lowered his voice confidentially, as if afraid of being overheard. "We've been chatting with some of the staff about those hidden cameras someone's been putting in the guest rooms."

My ears pricked up. "Yeah?"

"We've got some pretty reliable info about where the cameras are, but because guests are always in the rooms whenever we're at work, it's impossible for either of us to go into the rooms to retrieve them. Look." Chris took a pen and scrap of paper from his pocket and started to scribble on it, drawing a box. "Say this represents the bed in the apartment where Rihanna is currently staying…"

From memory, I started to visualise the apartment. It was on the first floor, in the far right corner of the building, with a private lift and back entrance, and the windows overlooked some offices and a side street. Even though I had only been into the apartment a few times, it was a very memorable space, and as it was the size of a large two-bedroomed flat, it was easy to picture yourself living there for a length of time. The wallpaper was a rich maroon, and it had an open-plan living/dining/kitchen area with a bedroom area at the end. A fairly long corridor led to the bathroom, with a second bedroom just off to the right. The only thing I didn't like about this apartment was that there was no partition separating the first bedroom from the living room. Why have a bedroom integrated into a living room when it's spacious enough to be a two-bedroomed flat?

Leaving all that aside, I brought my attention back to Chris and his sketch.

"And this is on the wall next to the bed." Chris drew

another box. Looking up, he said, "My drawing is rubbish, but does this make sense to you, Paul?"

"Yes," I replied. "Go on."

"Well, there's a mini camera hidden inside the artwork on the wall above the bed."

I swore softly under my breath. I clearly remembered all the things on the wall in that room: there was a picture and also a sort of shallow wooden display box, with a pane of glass covering the front, divided up into several little compartments, with different trinkets inside each. My favourite item in that display was a little silver thimble that reminded me of my grandma. That box was one of those things that caught your eye whenever you went into the room. It was art, I suppose, although personally, I couldn't really understand the thinking behind it. Just one of those quirky design features that the interior designer had placed in the room for intrigue and quaintness.

"The camera's in a difficult place and it won't be easy to remove discreetly," Chris explained. "I'll need some time to do it and some tools."

I gave it some consideration. Letting a security man into a celebrity's personal suite for some period of time – especially the suite of a celebrity with a cohort of PAs and other assistants and hangers-on – was not going to be easy. There had to be a better way.

Chris and Marc then started to debate where the cameras were in Michael Bublé's suite. "After comparing the information we've received from all our different sources, we reckon there are two cameras in his room," Marc said.

"Huh?"

That just didn't make any sense to me. As far as I was concerned, Michael Bublé was the least interesting celebrity staying at the hotel. He seemed downright dull, compared with some of the wild people we catered for. Rihanna's room had one camera in it, and she was a prime object of interest. Why put two cameras in Michael Bublé's room, of all people? Then again, the room layout and design were different, so that might have played a part in the spies' decision on exactly where they should hide a miniature camera to get the widest, most interesting and scandal-worthy footage.

So there were, allegedly, three hidden cameras, in the rooms of two major celebrities. We needed to get rid of them all without anyone knowing. I came to the only decision possible.

"Where are the cameras?" I asked. "Think I could take them all out? That would be more discreet than you going into the guests' rooms." If I was caught in there, guests would object less to finding a manager doing an emergency spot-check than to a security man in their room unannounced.

"Seems there's a clock with a hidden camera in it on the bookshelf," Chris said, sketching some more lines and boxes. "And another, under the coffee table, placed at an angle so that it surveys his bed. D'you think you could get them?"

I nodded, thinking it through. "Yeah. Why not?" I said. "If it came down to it, it's better for me to be found in a guest's room than you."

"OK," he said, checking my face to see how serious I was about this. I was. Very. "So, what you need to bear in mind is this..." He went on to explain exactly what I had to do.

I took it all in, committing it to memory. "Right!" I slapped both hands decisively down on the table-top to seal the deal. "Let's do it."

We agreed it would be my task to retrieve the cameras when I returned to work that night. I enjoyed the rest of my brunch in Chris and Marc's company before setting off home.

On my journey back to my flat, I was in a reflective mood, still wondering what it was that Steph wanted to tell me. I had hopes, of course, that she would be telling me that she wanted me... that we should go out for a drink... a romantic meal... get to know one another better. Or that she couldn't live without me. That she had been trying to keep a lid on her feelings because she didn't like to mix work with pleasure, but she just couldn't resist any more. That she had realised she wanted me just as much as I wanted her. That she had split up from her partner...

My imagination kept me busy all the way home. There were so many scenarios to consider, and I couldn't wait to find out what Steph meant. I kept checking my phone to see if she had contacted me again, but I didn't want to harass her by texting her. I would wait for her to tell me. As soon as I got home, I showered to rid myself of work and all its misery, then went straight to bed.

Arriving back at work that evening, I hoped Steph would be there. She wasn't.

"Seen anything of Steph?" I asked Nicolas, the events manager when I bumped into him.

"No, I haven't." He shook his head, grimacing awkwardly.

"D'you know if she's been in at all today?"

"I don't believe she has. But I think *something*'s going on," he looked at me pointedly.

I frowned at him. What did he mean?

He went on to say, "I've heard rumours that

Stephanie and some of the other managers and directors are going to be sacked, or moved to another property."

"What?" I was aghast. "Wow! Are you serious?"

I was shocked. What would I do if I never saw Stephanie again? If I didn't work with her every day? I couldn't believe it. No! I didn't want to believe it. I pondered for a few seconds, recovering myself, then wondered aloud, "Why all the changes?"

Nicolas pulled a face, shrugging. "If we're not reaching our financial and service standard targets, they usually do a reshuffle of the managers within the company, to get things back on track," he replied.

"Uh-huh," I nodded, trying to be restrained, whilst inside, I was screaming, *Oh, my God!* But it wasn't a done deal, yet. I calmed myself down and breathed evenly, deciding I would control my panic until I knew for sure. "So... What's the rationale, there?"

Nicolas rolled his eyes. "Well, you know Dana..."

We continued to give our opinions on the way the company was being managed and just as we got onto talking about the morning briefing, my phone rang.

"Sorry, Nicolas. Excuse me," I said, clicking on my phone.

"Hello, Paul." The call was from the switchboard operator, who explained that there was a lady on the phone who claimed to be the wife of Mr Brady, one of our regular guests. "Mrs Brady says she needs to speak to the manager in charge. She said it's a complaint about one of our staff. She doesn't sound very happy."

"OK, then," I said. "Put her through. Sorry," I mouthed to Nicolas, my hand over the phone's microphone. "I'd better take this."

Nicolas raised a hand in farewell and left me to get on with my phone call. I nodded gratefully at him and took a deep breath as the line clicked through. "Hello, Mrs Brady. How are you?"

"To whom am I speaking?" The tone was sharp; stern. Angry, even.

"You are speaking to Paul. I am the manager in charge. How may I help you this evening?" I asked, in the most charmingly polite tone of voice I could muster.

"Do you know my husband?" she asked, tersely. "John Brady?"

Although I was a relative newcomer myself, I did know Mr Brady. Even in the short time I had been at the Hotel Mannequin, he had stayed there almost every week when on business trips to London, often for a few days at a time. He had been a frequent guest at the hotel over a number of years, as I understood it.

"Oh, yes," I replied to her. "I know him very well, Mrs Brady."

"And do you know one of your staff – a slut called Dana Walsh?"

I gulped. On hearing Dana's name, my voice went a little shaky. "Yes, I do," I replied, quietly.

Mrs Brady's voice, in contrast, grew stronger and angrier. "Well, you know what?" she yelled. "I am a married woman with kids, and I don't know who this bitch Dana thinks she is..." By now, she was screaming down the phone. "But you'd better tell her to get her filthy hands off my husband!"

My eyes must have been as wide as saucers. But I could only listen in silence to her tirade of venom and accusations against Dana Walsh. Whoa! My ears were burning with the heat of her words, even over the phone. If this was all true, what I was hearing was pure gold.

"I want you to fire her!" she went on. "She's sleeping with hotel guests, including my husband! I've got an email she sent to him, here in front of me, asking for a Chanel handbag – and the rest!" She started to sob.

"Mrs Brady..." I began, in what I hoped was a soothing tone. But I couldn't get any more words out, because she had only paused for breath and to cry for a second or two, before launching again into an angry outburst.

"And you know what?" she shrieked. "*I* don't even own a fucking Chanel handbag! I spend my days looking after our children while this bitch is sleeping with my husband and taking what little money he has, money that should be used to look after us!"

I tried to get a word in, but the way she was ranting and screaming it wasn't easy. I waited till she ran out of steam, hearing all manner of details I didn't really think I wanted to know. But they were all very interesting, nevertheless, and I mentally filed them away for future reference.

Finally, having thought up an appropriate approach, I got a chance to speak. "I'm Dana Walsh's boss," I lied, making my voice sound firm and authoritative. "Rest assured, I will deal with her and put a stop to whatever she's doing, Mrs Brady. Leave it with me and I will sort it out in the morning."

For another half an hour, Mrs Brady continued to express her disbelief at what Dana was doing. She also insisted on reading out to me the email that Dana had sent to her husband, word for word. Oh, my God! No wonder she was upset! From the explicit content of that email, what was going on between Dana and Mr Brady was undeniable, and I was genuinely shocked.

Bloody hell! I couldn't believe that this was the same manager who routinely berated me and the other managers for unprofessional behaviour! And yet, here she was, clearly busy shagging the guests, all that time. What a bloody hypocrite!

Stunned, I walked back to the office and sat down to take it all in. My mind was reeling with all this information. There was part of me that wanted to laugh out loud, long and hard, in amazement and delight. Or to turn around and gossip to the nearest staff: "OMG! You'll never guess what I've just heard!" But then... I thought again. Oh, this was brilliant! This was explosive! Just the sort of ammunition I needed!

I was suddenly aware that I was grinning away to myself. My facial expression must have gradually changed from one of preoccupied concern whilst I was first listening to Mrs Brady, to delirious joy with the increasing realisation of the power this information gave me over my nemesis. My mind was busy turning it all into a cunning plan that should make my life a whole lot better.

I decided that I would make sure I had a one-to-one with Dana when she arrived at work in the morning. Then I could use my conversation with Mrs Brady for the leverage I needed to get Dana off my back. This was perfect! It might just allow me to stay on working there, earning this great money and doing my job well, without feeling constantly criticised, persecuted and humiliated.

However, before I got to that point, there was still this shift to do, and my secret mission to fulfil. I still had a spy camera to decommission and dismantle without being seen. I might not be Bond, James Bond, but my mission was one of counter-espionage. I still had to retrieve and destroy the cameras from the rooms where Rihanna and Michael Bublé were staying.

It was just over an hour after my interesting phone call from Mrs Brady when Carl, the concierge, rang me. "Evening Paul. Just calling to inform you that Rihanna and her entourage are going out to dinner and will be leaving in fifteen minutes."

It was standard practice for staff to alert me to the comings and goings of our VIP guests – to enable us to be on hand, to alert security and manage the press photographer, for one thing. On this particular night, however, this news was also my trigger to action, my signal for preparing myself to access Rihanna's – hopefully – empty suite.

"Thanks, Carl. That's great." Adrenalin started surging through my system as I geared myself up for the task ahead. I just had to wait until they were all safely off the premises. I was, like Bond's Martini, shaken, but not stirred.

I was already prepared as far as equipment was concerned, since I'd collected the essential items together that made up the toolbox I was planning to use to recover the cameras, and had it to hand. But this was going to be tricky. Even though Rihanna and her entourage were going out, she sometimes left one or two people behind in her suite, including a security guard. I needed to be mindful of that, and prepared for this eventuality.

I also let Chris and Marc in the security office know what was happening so they could be on the lookout. "I'm going to try her suite once they are out of the hotel. Just keep an eye open for any press photographer preventing Rihanna and her entourage from leaving – or anything else that might delay their departure."

"Yes, we'll be sure to watch out," said Marc. "And if they come back suddenly, we'll call you straight away."

I laughed. "You better had!"

Thirty minutes went by, but it was no surprise that they were late. It was bad enough waiting for one 'ordinary' woman when she was getting ready to go out, let alone an A-list celebrity whose every movement was followed by the press photographer, and who was judged by the world on her appearance and actions. You couldn't expect a pop star with the high expectations, perfect looks and reputation of Rihanna to be able to just nip out at the drop of a hat. Not to mention her dozens of PAs, make-up artists, hairstylists and army of other followers. Going out was like preparing for battle. It just didn't happen within fifteen minutes. So, although I was buzzing with anticipation, I would just have to sit it out. Meanwhile, I waited around at the concierge desk in the lobby, spoke to several guests and answered a few of the calls that came in; just biding my time.

After about forty-five minutes, Rihanna's PA approached the concierge desk, deep in conversation on her mobile phone. I couldn't help but notice how stunningly dressed she was. She can't have been any taller than five feet five inches, but the heels of her boots gave her an additional six inches, making her almost as tall as me.

I overheard her saying into the phone, "Yeah. You can pull up at the front. We're ready to go."

She was immaculately stylish. When she clicked off her phone, it was impossible for me to resist complimenting her. "May I just say how stunning you look, madam? I especially love the boots."

She practically looked through me; her reply was just a small pressing together of her heavily-glossed lips, as if to say, "Yeah, I know I'm gorgeous. But don't talk to me." She might as well have lifted her palm and said, "Talk to the hand."

Moments after she'd finished the call, I noticed two black Mercedes S-class cars with tinted windows pulling up at the hotel's main entrance. They would all be leaving very soon, which would be my alert to spring into action. But I couldn't concentrate on that thought for long, since my view was interrupted by the looming figure of another guest who had come to the concierge desk.

"Could you get us a reservation tonight, please?" smiled a middle-aged man in glasses. "Somewhere like a jazz bar?"

"Certainly sir." I snapped back into my professional duties. "What time, please?"

"About nine-thirty?" he suggested, pushing the frame of his glasses up the bridge of his nose with his index finger.

"Certainly sir."

I was just looking through our contacts list and about to make a call when I spotted a group of six people, including Rihanna herself, walking regally through the lobby towards the main entrance, about to leave the hotel. I stopped what I was doing, frozen in mid-movement, and just gawped at her, completely entranced. This was the spell she cast wherever she went. If you have never seen Rihanna up close, you won't really know what I am talking about, but she just has a 'presence'. An aura of confidence and importance emanates from her, and she is a vision of delicate beauty. For me, when she appeared, it was as if a heavenly choir had suddenly burst into life, while everything went into slow motion and soft focus. What really did it for me were her eyes, her ass and her hips. From the fluidly smooth way she moved you would have thought she was floating, rather than walking like a common human being. She was like an angel. But so curvaceous and sexy! Others in her procession of 'people' danced attendance on her, and more of her team emerged from the lift and hurried to catch up with the main group, and with their mistress. Rihanna was the still, calm centre of focus for the parade of pampering minions bustling around her. Astonishingly gorgeous and powerful, she strode onwards, the empress of all she surveyed. My mind was completely derailed.

All this might seem an exaggeration, but it was true. I realised I wasn't breathing – she had literally taken my breath away. Maybe my heart had stopped beating, too, lost as I was in that moment of eternity. I should just go and lie on the ground in front of her and tell her to walk over me, I thought. *Rihanna, use me as you will. Wipe the dirt off your shoes on me. Anything.* What a woman!

When she disappeared outside and the group got into the waiting cars, I finally remembered to breathe again. I was at last able to close my mouth and come back to consciousness. I spotted Marc at the door, giving me a knowing stare. My trance had only lasted a matter of seconds, but it had felt much longer: timeless.

I snapped out of it and got back to making the reservation for the other guest. The sooner I did this, the sooner I could hurry off to Rihanna's suite and remove that camera. I managed to get the guest and his partner a booking at the jazz club, which pleased him no end.

After thanking me, he asked: "Was that Rihanna?"

"It was." She hadn't booked under an assumed name, and it seemed churlish to lie, especially when the evidence was pretty obvious.

"Amazing! Do you get a lot of celebrities here? It is a lovely hotel..." He launched into a conversation about the hotel, evidently in the mood for a chat. I answered politely, but it seemed that it was going to be a long conversation, so I had to interject. "I'm so sorry, sir, but there is a matter I have to deal with for Rihanna, and I must complete it before she gets back. I hope you have a wonderful evening."

"Oh... oh, yes. Of course," said the guest reluctantly, his face dropping, slightly caught off balance by my polite dismissal. He pushed up his glasses, and peered at me, saying, "Thank you."

I left him standing there, turned into the back office and grabbed my little toolbox. The private lifts to Rihanna's and other apartments were on the other side of my office, which meant that at least I didn't need to go back into the lobby and encounter chatty-man again, or anyone else who might nobble me and impede my progress.

I slipped out of the office and took the lift. Within seconds, I was on the first floor, walking towards the Apartment Two. I knocked and rang the doorbell twice, straining my ears to listen, just to make sure there was nobody in. No response.

Opening the door with my key, I stepped in cautiously. A wall of hot, dry air immediately hit me, taking my breath away and practically singeing my eyebrows. It was very obvious that Rihanna, coming from Barbados, must have liked the temperature that way, because the room was so swelteringly hot that you could almost imagine you were in the Caribbean.

"Hello?" I called out querulously, just in case there was anyone in the bedroom or bathroom, out of sight. "It's duty maintenance!" I paused, listening for any response, then shouted out again, "I've come to check on the coffee machine!"

All the lights were off, except for the one in the corridor. I repeated my "duty maintenance" call as I stepped further into the open-plan living space.

"Hello?"

Nothing. I breathed out in relief. As far as I *could* actually breathe, in that atmosphere. It was stifling.

Flicking on the light in the living room, I walked towards the bed where Rihanna slept, picking my way through an obstacle course of empty or half-full designer shopping bags and discarded shoes. This was the thing that really struck me – the number of clothes and things lying heaped around the place. I know they had asked for hundreds of clothes hangers, but it seemed they needed even more. Really, they could have done with another apartment just for her stuff!

God, but it was roasting hot in there. I felt trussed up like a turkey in that tropical climate, so I took off my jacket, placing it carefully on a chair, and immediately felt some relief. I could clearly see the wooden display box on the wall, with the trinkets in it. *OK*, I thought, *I need to be quick. But how do I do this?*

I felt around the edges of the wooden box to see if I could take it down from the wall easily, then open the glass cover, without everything falling out. I had a vain hope that it might be hung like a painting on a hook. But no. It didn't move at all. Maybe it was screwed to the wall with mirror-plates. Sweat was running into my eyes, and I had to loosen my tie and open a couple of shirt buttons. The temperature was blistering, and I felt sick enough with tension, even without this intense heat. No good – it became apparent that taking down the entire display case wasn't an option: apart from the whole thing looking really heavy, an unusual screw-like fitting inside it had been used to attach it to the wall. My only choice would be to leave it all up, but take off the glass front, which was screwed into place.

I wiped the back of my hand over my forehead, but it did no good, really. Even the back of my hand was moist. I was feeling clammy all over, and the sensation of sweat dripping down my spine did nothing to help.

I peered in through the glazed front of the display case, cupping my hands around my eyes to deflect the glare of the lights reflected on the glass. Scrutinising each of the compartments with their intriguing items, at first glance I couldn't see anything that looked like a camera. But on closer inspection, I could tell that one particular trinket in one of the small compartments didn't accord with the others. *Gotcha!* No bigger than an AAA battery, this particular item stood out from the rest because it was new and made of black plastic, whereas all the other items, including an old matchbox and my favourite thimble, were vintage and made of metal or cardboard. *Right.* I was ready.

I opened the toolbox and saw almost immediately that I didn't have the right size of screwdriver to open the box's glass cover. "Crap!" I cried out loud. I ran over to the apartment's small kitchen and opened the drawers to see what size knives were in there. Shucking the cutlery around with a metallic rattle, I picked out a selection. I inspected four different sized knives, including a silver dinner knife, planning to take them all over to the display case on the far wall.

"OK, surely one of these will do," I muttered. Licking my lips, I tasted a salty tang from the streams of sweat coursing down my face.

Rushing back to the bedroom area, I tried the first knife, which didn't work. It was just not strong enough. Sweat was literally dripping from my brow and splashing onto the surfaces below, with the heat, exertion and stress of it all. *So much for leaving no traces of DNA,* I thought. *I'll never make a proper burglar.* Testing out each knife, it soon became clear that only the silver dinner knife looked to be up to the job. Painstakingly, I was able to insert the tip of the knife blade into the groove and begin to unscrew one of the fixings of the display case's glazed front.

Whoever had put the camera in the box in the first place must have encountered the same problem as I did. The camera had been placed in the top left-hand corner of the box, evidently so that just the corner of the glass could be pulled apart and the camera could be put in and taken out without having to take the entire glass face off. Once I was able to loosen the screws that held the glass in place in that corner, it was simple to ease the panel forward a little and slip my hand inside to retrieve the camera between my fingers. I pocketed the tiny machine and screwed the display case's front panel back on.

Phew! Thank God that was over. My heart was pounding and I was drenched in sweat. My wet shirt was stuck to my skin as if I'd worn it to go swimming in the pool. I tidied up and returned the knives to the kitchen drawer, grabbing my jacket and giving one last glance around the apartment to make sure that I was leaving everything just as it had been when I arrived. Then I switched off the light.

I swiftly left the apartment, relieved to breathe in the relatively cool air of the air-conditioned hallway. I headed back to the office, this time via the back stairwell rather than using the private lift again. I was keen to get out of the way as quickly and as surreptitiously as possible. Still sweating and a little shaken, I was buzzing with adrenaline. What if I'd been caught? Everyone would think I'd put the cameras there in the first place, and was coming back to collect the evidence. Thank God I had got away with it.

I was still shocked that somebody had been able to place a surveillance camera in a guest's room in the first place. Maybe hotels should have had a better internal security checking systems or standard procedures for this kind of thing, but I guess that if the person who was responsible for checking the rooms was also the one putting the cameras or other malicious items in there in the first place, there wasn't all that much that could be done to rectify the matter.

I have to say, what surprised me most about the whole thing was the slackness of Rihanna's own security team. You would have thought a celebrity of her calibre would have had her security guards carry out a thorough search of the room before she arrived. They were careful and demanding enough about other things. After all, devices to prevent security breaches are readily available – for example, all kinds of equipment are used in cinemas to detect the illicit recording of pirate videos by unscrupulous audience members. Besides, the rooms in the hotel were minimalist and uncluttered – at least before Rihanna's shopping and stuff had got in there. There weren't many places to hide things in the room, so it would have been an easy task for her security just to do an initial sweep of the place.

With the tiny camera burning a hole in my pocket, I also couldn't help wondering what was recorded on it. Hopefully, something that was worth all the sweat and panic I'd suffered trying to get it out! Anything with Rihanna on it would be a bonus. To me, let alone to whoever had rigged it up, presumably in the hope of picking up enough information or scandal to sell to the media. I would soon see, anyway.

Returning to the back office, I stuck my head around the door to the lobby and gave Marc the thumbs-up signal to acknowledge that Mission One was complete. He gave a nod of approval and grinned back at me.

One down, one to go, I thought. We planned to remove the camera from Michael Bublé's room the next night. One surreptitious mission per night was enough for me – and all my system could take.

Besides, I doubted whether another night there would do much harm or get much that would be worth selling to the press.

I kept the camera in my pocket as the night continued, since I planned to take it home with me, where I could view it privately without fear of anyone walking in and seeing it. However, I let my accomplices know that I would download the footage when I got home and I promised I would make copies for them, too.

But Marc was desperate to see the footage for himself. "It's Rihanna!" he said, shrugging and turning his palms up in a pleading gesture.

"In the privacy of her own bedroom!" Chris said, adding almost apologetically, "What's not to like? What can you do?"

Somehow I didn't think they were going to be so keen to see the Michael Bublé footage.

As usual, the rest of the night was far from peaceful. It was standard practice for the hotel to have a reduced housekeeping service after 11pm, which left me to manage the two or three staff still on duty. We had received numerous requests from guests during the evening, including some demands for ironing services, a change of bedding, and a manicure set, all adding pressure to the overstretched housekeeping service. It got so hectic that I had to get involved and help out wherever help was needed. I even ended up cleaning rooms. At one point, I seemed to be running from department to department non-stop.

One of the housekeeping staff in particular, Andy, was always a problem to work with. He could never be completely trusted to carry out a task, and he often appeared distracted. Sometimes he even seemed to be drunk. I really needed the staff to be fully focused and fully functioning – especially on this shift – but as far as Andy was concerned, that night was no different from any other.

On this occasion, I bumped into Andy in the lobby and asked him, "Did you complete that task I gave you earlier?"

He turned his acne-scarred face towards me. "What task?" he replied, sullenly.

"I asked you to clear up the vomit reported in the bathroom of room 104."

"You must be joking!" he sneered, turning his back on me. He walked off in the direction of the back office, which gave access to the events areas and housekeeping office.

"Andy!" I was furious and followed him into the back office, shouting out, "Stop! I need to talk to you!"

He continued to ignore me, crossing the room.

Fuming at his insolence, I hurried after him towards the housekeeping office, which he entered, closing the door on me behind him. There was no way I was going to stand for this. I ran over to the housekeeping office door and followed him in. I found him standing between the piles of bags of bedding that were waiting to be ironed.

"What's your problem, Andy?" I cried, my blood pumping with exertion and anger. "I asked you a question and I need an answer. I asked you twenty minutes ago to clean room 104. Have you done it?"

He didn't answer at first, just gave me a dull, blank stare as he slowly shook his head. Then, as if in a sudden psychotic twist of personality, he completely snapped.

"Fuck you!" he yelled, his face ugly with venom. "I'm not doing shit!"

He swayed sideways where he stood, having to shuffle to regain his footing. He was clearly off-balance, almost falling over. His hand shot out, using the shelves full of laundry equipment and supplies to prop himself up.

"Have you been drinking?" I asked him.

"No," he laughed. But the laugh went on for far too long, his fleshy lips leering. "Ha-haa-haaa-haaaa!"

"You must have had something to drink," I

repeated, furious. "You look drunk." His smile froze, then dropped completely as his gaze wandered. "And did you clear room 420?" I continued to question him, but he ignored me. "Have you done *anything* at all that you've been asked to do, tonight?"

"I am going to fuck you up!" he roared, suddenly lunging towards me with a steam iron held in his fist, swung backwards. "Just leave me alone!"

Jeez! Within a split-second, I instinctively stepped back, reaching out to protect myself from his attack. I grabbed a metal pole from one of the dismantled clothes rails that were leaning against the wall, and snapping into the defensive stance of a ninja warrior, I held it up in front of me in both hands like a martial arts weapon.

"You might fuck me up," I snarled through gritted teeth, "but I will *kill* you. Do you *know* me, cunt?"

He blinked at me, twice, and immediately stopped in shock, the iron still raised high in his hand, realising that intimidating me wouldn't work. He took a step backwards, the weight of the iron above his head causing him to fall back against the wall, which he slid down, before crumpling onto the ground like a cartoon character and letting the iron drop form his grasp.

As soon as he had moved away from me, I had reached for the phone and called for security:

"Housekeeping office. Now!"

Appreciating the urgency of my tone, Chris, the security guard, soon arrived, and found me still brandishing my metal pole like a **Bōjutsu stick-fighter** and standing over my defeated opponent. Andy was sitting slumped against the wall, his limbs loose like a broken-stringed puppet. The iron was tossed aside next to him, its electrical lead looping across the floor. Chris's face frowned, and he looked at me questioningly. I could tell he couldn't figure out if there had been an accident or a fight. Some laundry-related accident or an ironing, clothes-hanging fight.

I instructed Chris: "Escort this man off the hotel premises, please."

Without any further ado, Chris immediately hauled Andy up from where he was sitting on the floor, and I addressed his dazed, spotty face while Chris apparently held Andy's whole weight upright by his arms. I was still shaking with fury, my mouth set in a snarl.

"Don't bother returning to work. Ever," I told Andy, in disgust. "The Human Resources Department will be in touch."

Chris took Andy to his locker so that he could get changed and pick up his belongings. He would then be escorted out of the hotel.

I was left there amongst the cleaning equipment, panting and bewildered, trying to take it all in. I'd never had to deal with a situation like that before, or had any training in what to do when faced with that kind of aggression. I wasn't sure if I'd responded in the correct manner, or what I could have done differently – it was so difficult to gauge. No doubt Dana would call me grossly unprofessional, but, faced with a guy about to bash my brains out with a heavy iron, I hoped I was allowed to be something less than a polite model manager. I straightened my tie and tugged down my jacket, composing myself.

Chris returned to the housekeeping office to find me still standing there. He asked, staring at me wide-eyed in amazement, "What went on there then?"

I told him everything that had occurred, ending with: "Looked like he was pissed out of his head."

"Stoned, more like." I looked at Chris questioningly, so he explained: "Andy is always smoking marijuana on his breaks. I've spoken to him about it on more than one occasion. Didn't say anything to any of the managers, though, because I didn't want to get him into trouble."

I raised one eyebrow and shook my head in disbelief. "God's sake, Chris…"

Needless to say, Chris really should have told one of us – at least, me. That it had come to this!

I returned to the back office, pondering on what had happened and wondering exactly how I should word my report to the director. Bloody hell! Taking drugs at work – on the premises, or at least, on his breaks! That explained a lot of things about Andy. His attitude on many occasions. His slapdash approach to work. His glazed, out-of-it expression. Let alone a violent outburst like that, which was bad enough as it was, but could have been so much worse. If only Chris had said something. But I couldn't really blame him. We couldn't depend on other staff grassing up their colleagues, I suppose.

That incident got me thinking that perhaps companies like ours should include random drugs tests as part of their staffing policies. I couldn't help thinking how much worse this situation might have been. And not just for me, on this particular occasion. What would have happened if Andy had become aggressive with one of the guests? Or, in a worst-case scenario, what if a member of staff killed themselves – or someone else – whilst under the influence of drugs? An innocent guest, for example? It didn't bear thinking about. This was going to be another subject for debate at the morning briefing.

There was a lot going on in my head that night, which unsettled me. It had been a thoroughly unpleasant evening, although once again I had done my very best to handle it. And yet, regardless of what I did, nobody in senior management seemed to appreciate my efforts. Coupled with that, not seeing Stephanie or having any interaction with her was getting to me. My mood was low, and I was frustrated that things were not in my control and I could apparently do nothing to make them any better. Except that I was now more than ready to see if I could use the leverage I had over Dana to get some respect from her, and some respite from her constant barrage of criticism and negativity.

Guest check-out that morning was really busy and I had to provide support for the reception staff to keep things running smoothly without delays for the guests. There's nothing worse than finishing your stay at a hotel and having to wait in a queue to complete a laborious checking-out procedure. Consequently, I was stuck at the desk for over two hours as the flow of departing guests continued unabated.

I had just checked out yet another guest and was about to tidy up the paperwork when I saw a taxi pull up outside. And Dana stepped out of it. My breath caught in my throat.

She's early, I thought. I was momentarily caught off-guard, but I scrabbled my thoughts together and braced myself for what I had planned to do next. I would be breezy and professional, but direct.

As she was carefully placing her high heels on each step with a click, descending the flight of low marble steps that led to the oak-wood lobby, I dashed out from behind the desk to meet her.

"Good morning, Dana! How are you?" I said.

She looked at me oddly, with knitted brows, as if wondering what the hell was wrong with me, greeting her in such a friendly, effusive manner. She said, "Good morning" without a break in her pace, strutting onwards, muttering, "I'm fine."

I followed, trying to catch her up, addressing her back as she advanced purposefully away from me. I called after her: "I received a call last night from Mr Brady's wife."

Even from the back, I could see Dana's horrified reaction. She froze to the spot, her shoulders tense. She slowly turned first her head, and then her body, to face me.

"What?" she whispered, her face taut. She gave me no eye contact – just jerked her head sideways, indicating for me to follow her.

With a more determined stride, she approached her

office. "Come in Paul," she said primly, still avoiding looking at me.

We walked through her PA's office and into the more secluded space of her own private office, with her luxurious desk and fixtures. She swung around to face me at last.

"What do you mean you got a call from Mr Brady's wife?" she snapped. Before I could answer her first question, a second and then a third followed rapidly: "At what time was this? What did she say?"

"She called during the early part of the night and asked to speak to the manager in charge, so I took the call," I said innocently, my face impassive, even though I was smirking on the inside. "I'll be straight with you," I went on. "She basically called to say that you were shagging her husband and she wanted you to lose your job."

I paused to take in Dana's response. Her mouth hung open in shock, but I pressed on. "She forwarded an email to me that you'd sent Mr Brady, asking for a Chanel handbag, amongst other things. But I don't need to go into all that - you know what's in the email. You wrote it." Dana looked stunned but said nothing. I continued: "Mrs Brady was in tears. She said you're a whore and a slut and she thinks you want to take her husband and the father of her children from her, and she told me there's no way she'll allow you to do so. She made it pretty clear that she's going to come after you and make sure you lose your job."

Dana slumped down into her chair and held her head in her hands. She was no longer the powerful, aggressive person she had always portrayed herself as in our briefings. I was really enjoying this.

"I told her I was your boss. I said I would take care of the matter and she could leave it with me."

Dana lifted her head and looked up. Her face was white with shock. "It's not what you think," she said, clearing her throat and trying to compose herself, although she was still clearly rattled. "I'm sorry you had to take all that from her. Thank you – I'll deal with it."

As I walked out through the oak-wood lobby to the back office, I had a huge grin on my face. Maybe I should have followed it through by capitalising on my leverage over her and demanding something from her in return for my silence, but I was a bit wary of her firing me on the spot. She was my boss, after all. To be honest, though, just letting her know that I knew what she was up to was enough. The look on her face had been priceless. And, I figured, this news might just be enough to get her off my back, and maybe it would offer a reason for her to finally give me some credit for my hard work. If she couldn't bring herself to do it out of professionalism or the goodness of her heart – if she had no goodness, and she had no heart – then maybe she would give me some credit in order to save her own skin.

That morning's briefing was very short. Dana came in, tight-lipped and brusque, and briefly explained that there would be a reshuffle of the senior managers and that we would see the changes in the coming days. That was it – she didn't say anything else, just turned on her heel and left.

I don't know if anyone else noticed it, but I could see the worry etched on Dana's face and she couldn't make eye contact with me at all. I felt victorious in some ways, but this was countered by the continued absence of Stephanie. From what Dana had just said about changes, it looked as if the rumours were true and Steph would be moved to another property. This was devastating news, if it turned out to be true. I was worried that I would never see her again. Was this going to be the end of our flirtation and the death of any chance of a romance with her?

I was tempted to text Steph, but I didn't know what to say. I didn't want to alarm her if she knew nothing about all these changes. I didn't even want to broach the subject. Basically, I had the strange belief that if I didn't talk about it, it wouldn't be true.

After the morning briefing had ended, I went home, knowing that I still couldn't relax; my work would be continuing even though I was off the clock. I had some special overtime to do – I needed to download the video from the camera from Rihanna's room, and watch it. Even though it was unpaid work, it was more like pleasure to me – and it was something I had been looking forward to. Hell, I would have paid somebody to let me do it!

I made a quick cup of tea and decided to forget about eating any breakfast, because this was too good to delay. Then I got my laptop ready for what I hoped would be the video of all videos.

I made myself comfortable on the sofa in my living room and placed the laptop and my cup of tea on the coffee table. *Oh, this should be good!* Taking a sip from my cup, I booted up the laptop, loosened my tie, and set to work. Getting the image files was really easy, since the camera had a tiny memory card, just like the ones used to add data space to smartphones. All I needed to do was slot the memory card into the laptop.

I stared at the screen, eager to see what the camera had picked up. It was trained on the bed area and I fast-forwarded through, because there was a fair amount of nothing much to see. But then... *Bingo!* I hit the mother lode. The video image was poor because the room was dark, but on the bed you could clearly see the glowing screen of a Mac laptop and an almost naked female lying down in front of it. I peered, closer, trying to make out the detail. Although it was a partial side view, it was clear that it was Rihanna, and that she was on a video call with someone. I could see it was a man, since I could see him on her laptop screen, although it was small and indistinct from that angle. I just couldn't make out who it was.

But what were they saying? I fiddled with the sound levels, but the audio was really poor, so you couldn't make out what they were talking about. I sat back and blew out a long breath, eyes wide. The footage was longer than I had expected. It was dynamite! I rewound to the beginning of the best scene and watched again. I was vaguely aware that my cup of tea was sitting next to me, getting cold. But frankly, who cared? Boys, if you'd seen the curves and contours of her body, you would go crazy too. That is as much as I will say!

I watched it over and over and over again to see if I could see more of her, or hear what she was saying and to whom she was talking. But I had no luck - only a professional studio would be able to make the video's resolution any better. And don't imagine that I didn't consider paying for that.

My mind was racing. This was real. Imagine what else I might have seen! A wicked thought then occurred to me. It would be so easy to just quietly put the camera back in its place, and capture even more footage of her. If I got caught in the act of replacing the camera, that who'd be the end of me. Would the security guys back me up?

The fewer people seen this, the better – but no one has, apart from me. No way was I going to share it with Marc and Chris. I would keep it to myself. Although I'd promised each of them a copy, I decided to swap the authentic memory card with a blank one and give that to them. I would tell them nothing was on the memory at all.

"Would you believe it? What a bummer!" I would say, crestfallen. "Wonder what happened? Perhaps we took the camera away too soon. Or the camera was faulty."

Some things are best kept private. This incident should be an eye-opener to all of us – living in a digital age, we must be aware. There is an adage "bushes have ears, walls have eyes".

CHAPTER NINE

At last Steph came into work. She seemed a little distant and less flirtatious, which really saddened me, especially after she'd sent that sexy picture.

"You said you had something to tell me?" I asked hopefully, one moment when I happened to catch her with nobody else around.

"Oh, never mind," she said sadly. "It isn't relevant now." And she swung off down the corridor, leaving me standing.

I was confused by the mixed messages I was receiving from her, but I didn't want to push it by confronting her about it. Oddly, our relationship seemed to deteriorate after I gave her the gift. I still did all I could to repay her for standing up for me in the meeting with Dana, though. I also tried to inject some romance into our lives, so I bought her a rose, and left little notes for her in areas I knew she would go into, including the safe and the stationery cupboard. But if anything, she only grew colder.

I went to see Marc and Chris, and told them the devastating 'news'. "Sorry, lads. That camera I retrieved from Rihanna's apartment had no footage." I presented them with the camera and the blank memory stick.

"You're joking!" gasped Marc.

"Oh, for fuck's sake," Chris said. "That's my night ruined."

We still planned to retrieve and destroy the cameras from Michael Bublé's suite that night. The shift continued at a steady pace and, as usual, there were numerous requests from guests to deal with, and a lot of celebrity movement in and out.

The international rock band The Killers, who were regular guests at the hotel, had arrived that day. In my opinion, these guys were the coolest, both on and off stage.

Whenever the band stayed at our hotel, they could count on me to set up our private screening room so they could watch a movie with their friends. Tonight was no different: they were in town, I bumped into them at the hotel bar, and there was no question that I would go out of my way for them.

"Hey, Paul!" Ronnie Vannucci greeted me, clapping my hand into his. "How you doin'?"

We chatted a while, Ronnie's hands waving wildly in his characteristic enthusiasm to tell me the latest. But if I ever complimented him on their success, he was self-effacing and almost shy about it.

After setting up the screening room and making sure the band were comfortable, I set off on a floor security check. This regular walk was not only to make sure that Marc and Chris were doing their checks properly, but also to make sure that all the lifts, extinguishers and other equipment were in place and in working order. The best route was always for me to start off on the roof area and work my way down to the basement.

Checking off everything, it was clear that the roof and all the equipment up there were OK, so I moved down to the fifth floor. As I approached the premier suites (each reserved at a cost of over £4,000 per night), I heard loud music, talking and screaming laughter. It sounded like a party was in full swing.

I knew that the people in this particular suite

weren't celebrities. The Calvalis, as they called themselves – we didn't know their real name – were wealthy guests who would always book the top suites and several other rooms whenever they were in London, a whole floor if they could. They didn't worry about the expense at all; they always splashed out their cash whenever they stayed, without a care. In fact, they didn't really care about much at all, except for their own hedonism and fun. Their disregard for everyone else in the hotel was really quite unbelievable. Tonight was evidently just another party night for them, which usually meant lots of noise – and gorgeous half-naked women wandering around. The Calvalis would always reserve adjoining suites so that they could move freely between them. This was almost fundamental to their every booking, and the reason was clear: the girls would often wander through from room to room almost naked except for their underwear.

I followed the booming music and the chatter of what sounded like a hundred guests. As I approached the suite in question, I could see that the front door leading from the hotel corridor to their lounge was open. The music was extremely loud, loud enough to disturb other guests, and I decided to go and investigate.

As I walked into the bass-booming dimly-lit lounge,

I felt something soft land on my right shoulder, draped down onto my chest. Looking down, I could see that it was a white lacy padded push-up bra. Before I knew it, an even lighter piece of clothing hit my face, brushing against my lips as it slithered down my chin. Reaching up to catch it as it fell, I realised that it was a pair of very skimpy knickers. I dropped them on the floor and brushed off the bra, amazed.

The room was very dark, full of noise and black shadowy figures, and the music was way too loud. This was all too much.

I shouted "Excuse me!" but no one replied. They couldn't hear me. I had to switch on the main lights to get everyone's attention. There was a roar of surprise and a chorus of pained cries as the lights flared shockingly white and the guests blinked blindly at me. Silence fell before a further muttering of surprise and complaints began. Once the lights were on, however, the true level of debauchery became clear to me. It was a full-on orgy of sex, drugs, drinking and dancing. There was a half-naked couple having sex on the sofa, a naked threesome going on in the bedroom, and other people, in various stages of undress, were just kissing, fondling, dancing or drinking and smoking.

One of the Calvali brothers came over, grinning at

me, a crystal glass half-full of whisky in his hand. He raised his glass to me.

"Hi, governor!" he greeted me cheerfully. "I know it's a little bit noisy, but its Paolo's birthday and we're just showing him a good time." He gave me a wink. "He's in the main bedroom enjoying two ladies, and we would like to keep it that way." He looked at me pointedly, his grin never faltering.

These guests were a good source of income for the hotel, so I had to keep them sweet. "I don't mind them doing whatever they're doing," I said. "If they could just close the doors and turn the music down, it would be as though I never saw a thing."

"Sure thing," the Calvali brother grinned. He swung around, shouting, "Enzo! *Abbassare la musica!*" The music went a little quieter and Signor Calvali turned back to me. "Your wish is my command. Switch the light out on your way out, will you?"

"Of course."

As I turned to make my way out of the room, a slim, frisky-looking blonde wearing only lace knickers ran past me and slapped my bottom, laughing over her shoulder at me as she ran through the corridor and into one of the other rooms. I smiled, shaking my head slowly. I saw the humour in it all – if I hadn't had work commitments, it would have been nice to join in!

Continuing my rounds, as I made my way down the stairwell to the fourth floor, I called reception on my mobile, referring to Michael Bublé by the alias he used when he stayed with us. His suite was on the third floor, and I wanted to check that all was clear before I went in there to remove the cameras.

"I'm just ringing to find out if Mr Evans is in his room or in the hotel at all?"

The receptionist placed me on hold for a few seconds, then told me, "No, sorry Paul. He's not here. The concierge said he and his entourage left for Hammersmith about half an hour ago."

Convenient. Now was my chance. I decided to skip my check of the fourth floor and went straight down to the third. The sooner I did this, the better.

Bublé's junior suite, room 310, was right next to the stairwell, and as I turned the corner, I could see his door closing and a member of the housekeeping staff walking away from it towards the pantry. I approached the door and rang the doorbell.

"Yes? You can come in," came a voice from inside.

I jumped, but on the door was the housekeeping sign that read "Room is being serviced", so I knew it was probably another member of staff. I used my master key to open the door and entered.

"Hi Paul," said the room attendant, winding up the

lead of the vacuum cleaner, smiling up at me. "How are you?"

"Great, thanks." I looked carefully at her. To be honest, I couldn't remember her name, so I avoided using it. "It's been a long time since I last saw you."

"I've been on holiday in Tenerife," she answered, happily.

"Ah, that's why you're looking so rested, and with a lovely tan," I said, smiling.

She smiled back, resting her hand on the handle of the vacuum. "Can I help you with anything?"

"No," I replied, gazing around the room to see if I could pinpoint the cameras. The clock was pretty obvious to me – an unfamiliar, small black digital clock that wasn't part of our hotel provision or design sitting in full view. Still, you wouldn't think it had a camera inside. To a guest, it would just be part of the hotel décor, and if you worked in the hotel, you would have assumed it simply belonged to whichever guest was staying in the room. Either way, no one would think to be suspicious of it or touch it. Only I knew that it shouldn't have been there at all.

"No," I said breezily. "I'm just checking Mr Evans's room to make sure all the amenities are here." I added redundantly, perhaps overcompensating for appearing there rather unexpectedly, "You know, the usual stuff the duty manager does."

I walked over to the bedroom area and took in the perfectly-made king-sized bed with its crisp white linen. The simple art deco bedside table lamps cast pools of dim light. I couldn't immediately see any camera there, but I would have a good look around when the staff left.

I came back into the main room and perused the complimentary fruit bowl provided daily for Mr Evans's suite, as if a primary duty of the manager was to check that it held the required number of grapes.

The room attendant smiled. "OK, then," she said. "We're all finished here, so unless you need anything, I'd better go to the next room on my list."

"Maybe I'll see you later," I said, as she moved towards the door, trundling the vacuum cleaner before her.

"Bye, Paul."

As soon as she'd left, I picked up the clock that presumably held the camera and put it straight in my pocket, then started the hunt for the second camera, the one that was supposedly underneath the coffee table. I got down on my knees and looked under the table, but there was no sign of any hidden camera there. Maybe under something else? I checked under the TV stand in the living room area, but it wasn't there, either. Where the hell? I was beginning to think that the guys had got it wrong. The last place to look was under the TV stand in his bedroom. I peered underneath.

"Yes!" I whispered. "Got it!"

There, at the back, in the shadows, I could see a small black and silver device the size and shape of a lipstick on a tiny black stand screwed just under the lip of the TV stand's frame, out of sight. It had a lens on its pointed end, which just protruded below the TV stand's mahogany wooden top. The camera itself was even smaller than the one I'd removed from Rihanna's apartment. It looked as if it had been a rush job to install it, because the screws hadn't been completely secured.

I pulled on it, but at first it didn't budge. I yanked harder and twisted it, and it came loose. "OK, that's that," I murmured.

I stood up and placed it in my pocket with the clock. I still couldn't quite believe someone had done this, but my main concern now was to get out of the apartment and carry on with my duties as if nothing had happened. Fortunately, I encountered no one in the hallway outside, so I didn't even have to feign nonchalance.

Another treasure trove of video footage, I thought to myself as I headed for the lift. I wasn't looking forward to this one nearly as much as Rihanna's, though. As far as I knew Bublé always stayed in his room, and no "special guest" ever came to visit him at 2am, unlike so many of our male celebrity guests. In terms of ethics, morals, scandal and sexual appetite, Michael Bublé seemed more innocent than most choirboys. Why on earth would someone put a camera in *his* suite?

Still, it was for the best that I kept these things to myself.

On my way back to the office after completing my walkabout, I told Marc and Chris: "Nope. Nothing there."

"What?" asked Marc, frowning in puzzlement.

"I didn't find any cameras in the suite."

"Really?" exclaimed Chris in surprise. "Wasn't there a clock in there?"

"No. Nothing," I said firmly. Chris and Marc looked at one another in amazement. "Your sources must have been misinformed."

I left them gaping and went on, finishing my checks and then going over to the back office to work my way through the paperwork I still had to do. I sat down at my desk, picking up my pen, thoughtfully. The cameras were both still tucked in my pocket, and for some reason, I patted it for reassurance, feeling the small bulk still there. I smiled to myself, laughing at my apparent doubt. Did I think I might have been pickpocketed in the last hour? Not that this particular footage would be of any value to anyone. Not like the Rihanna tape!

Not long after I'd sat down at my desk, however, I received a call from Chris, asking me to come to the door where he was stationed.

"I've got a male here, claims to have been..." and here he lowered his voice discreetly. "...raped. Can you come and speak to him?"

"Raped?" I exclaimed, jumping to my feet. "Are you serious? Here?"

"No. Outside." Chris went on to explain that he wasn't a guest at the hotel, but he had approached Chris at the entrance, asking for help.

As I hurried out of the office, I could see Chris standing outside the door with a man in his twenties, smartly dressed, with dark brown hair and a fading tan. He looked shaken and somewhat frightened. As I approached Chris nodded, indicating that this was the man who was making the claim.

"Good evening," I said as I walked towards him. "My name is Paul, and I am the duty manager. My colleague told me you have a problem you need assistance with. How can I help you?"

The gentleman looked up at me, then his eyes darted from side to side, checking the entrance area and into the street. There was nobody else around within hearing distance, so he blurted out: "I've been raped." He swallowed hard and went on. "I can't believe this has happened to me," he said, almost apologetically. "I don't know what to do."

I answered him, I hoped, sympathetically. "Don't worry. I think the first thing we need to do is call the police. Maybe you would like a drink of water and somewhere to sit and wait?"

"Water would be a good start," he replied, "but I don't want to sit down, thanks. My bottom is really sore!" He winced, as if to demonstrate the fact.

"Oh, I see." I wasn't sure how to take this comment or what to do about it, but it was clearly a serious matter and I had to deal with it as such. "Please follow me." I invited the gentleman to come into the hotel and we went to a private event room that I knew was empty. I called the police and passed the phone to him to give details, whilst I stood discreetly aside, although I could still hear his conversation very clearly. It seemed that he had been raped at a nearby nightclub.

After speaking with the police for ten minutes or so, he handed the phone back to me, saying, "Where are we, exactly? Could you tell them? They want to know."

I told the police whereabouts in the hotel they could find us, and then we waited for them to arrive. The man stood there, occasionally sipping his glass of water nervously, but more often than not placing his glass on a table and anxiously wringing his hands, his slender fingers constantly moving.

"Do you live in London or are you staying nearby?" I asked.

"Why? Does this happen a lot around here?" he asked, his face stricken.

"No. Sorry, just making small talk."

It was an awkward situation - and yet another one that I'd never had to deal with before. Once the police arrived, I handed over to them and went back to the office.

It wasn't long before I received another call from security. "Paul. There's been a stabbing..."

"What?" I interrupted Marc.

"Just had a report of someone being stabbed, just outside the door of the hotel restaurant."

"Oh, my God! On our premises?"

"No. On the pavement just outside."

Bad as it was, I couldn't help breathing a sigh of relief that it hadn't been inside the hotel itself. But this was another serious situation I'd have to get involved in, which meant sitting down with the police and checking through the hotel's CCTV system recordings for video footage of the incident. Again.

By the time we had finished, I was sick of looking at video footage of any kind. I swear that if you had presented me with a new video of the naked Rihanna, I might have been hard pushed to drum up any enthusiasm. It was that bad. I was completely exhausted, after all the adrenalin that had been coursing through my veins all night, for one reason or another. I really felt as though I was running out of steam. And of course, concern about Stephanie was still on my mind, which darkened my outlook further.

Thankfully, the night finished much more quietly than it had started, and I was able do most of my admin and report writing unhindered for the rest of my shift. I left work early that morning and set off for home, feeling even more exhausted but looking forward to receiving my pay and bonus the next day. That was still a huge incentive for me to stay. After all this was over and I'd made myself a nice little pile of cash, I definitely needed a holiday.

I was so tired that I didn't even remember, until I got home, that I still had the cameras from Michael Bublé's suite to look at. I took them out of my pocket and looked at them sitting dully in the palm of my hand. I felt I couldn't be arsed. They certainly didn't motivate me as much as Rihanna's had. Who wanted to see Michael Bublé in his underpants? Certainly not me. Even if something unexpected had happened – an orgy with a legion of strippers or a team of cheerleaders – I was in no hurry to check, so I decided to leave them to view on my days off.

As the days went by, I eventually managed to get hold of all the spy cameras that were installed in the hotel. They revealed a great deal, and opened my eyes. There are many things that can be said, from video evidence and eyewitness accounts, but let's leave it there.

Finally I looked through Michael Bublé's tape. And what did I find? Absolutely nothing. Like the dedicated professional he clearly is, he had remained alone at all times, doing nothing more interesting than practising his scales. In contrast to the behaviour of most of our celebrity guests, and even the ordinary public, Michael Bublé was downright boring. I'm not sure it was really his sort of hotel, in fact. He seemed strangely out of place among the rest of them.

CHAPTER TEN

When I returned to the hotel, I discovered that the significant changes with managers that Dana had spoken about had already taken effect. A lot of the familiar managers had been moved elsewhere, and many departments had new ones in place. Some managers from the company's smaller properties had been promoted and were now working at Hotel Mannequin. And others had disappeared completely.

"Where's Steph?" I asked, trying not to sound too tremulous. Too interested. Too devastated.

"Haven't you heard?" said the events manager, Nicolas, who had somehow managed to stay in his role. It turned out that Stephanie had been moved to a smaller property – effectively, she had been demoted. On hearing this, I felt my chest tighten so that I could hardly breathe. My mind was full of questions, wonderings and conclusions. Although I had feared this might be the case – that what Nicolas had said about the company's shake-up might affect Steph – I had lived in hope. Even her coolness with me recently hadn't put me off. In fact, perhaps this was the reason for it. She had certainly been distancing herself from me, and I hadn't been able to understand it – until now.

It was a sad day for me, and for us all. The thought that I probably wouldn't see Steph again overshadowed my entire evening. Yet I pulled myself together, trying to concentrate on the evening handover that Nicolas was conducting. Numbly, I carried on listening as he confirmed: "You'll find that the morning briefing tomorrow will be different. All the new managers will be unveiled to you then."

I never imagined, as I arrived for my shift that evening, that something so awful was about to happen that it would change my view of life forever. Something that would affect me so deeply that my career and my own life would never be the same again.

The evening started off more quietly than usual,

ironically enough. There weren't many guests around; the bar and restaurant were doing steady business, although they were not as busy as they usually were. The night began with a couple of minor issues I had to deal with, but nothing out of the ordinary. Nothing on the scale of what was to happen later.

As I went on my rounds and chatted with some of the staff, one of my most trusted concierges, Les, came up to me. He looked distracted – agitated, even. With a hand on my arm, he led me aside to a quiet corner and spoke to me urgently and confidentially.

"I went to deliver an item to one of rooms, Paul. The male guest there pushed me down on the bed, unbuckled my belt, pulled down my trousers and gave me a blow job! No questions asked."

"Oh, my God!" I was pretty shocked, and with my thoughts reeling with the male rape the night before, I said, "Shit! We'd better call the police!"

"No, Paul – it's OK," Les told me, with an amused smile. "In the gay world, sex is a little bit more liberal. If someone wants to give you a blow job – well, why not?" He shrugged.

I stared at him. Really?

"Your face is a picture, Paul!" Les laughed. His eyes twinkled mischievously as he leant in to me and said, "Don't worry. I wasn't complaining about it. Boasting, more like!"

I went away, shaking my head in disbelief. Continuing on my rounds, Prita, another member of staff – a stunning brunette with a figure like a model - let on to me that she was in a relationship with one of our regular guests.

What was this? Staff sexual confession hour?

"During my break time in the evenings, I sneak up to Mr Higgs's room for a quickie," she said, her eyes gleaming with delight and sultry desire. "I take things up to his room as often as I can, so we can have long kisses."

"Really?" I said.

She leaned forward confidentially and told me, in a low voice, "A lot of the time, when I am at the desk, I am *wet*." She bit her lower lip and gazed at me, pointedly. "Dripping wet."

"Really?" I repeated. Was she coming on to me too? Otherwise, that was possibly too much information.

The funny part of this story, for me, was that Prita was 26 years old and stunning, whilst Mr Higgs was pushing 60, bespectacled and visually unappealing. He was also twice divorced and on his third marriage, with five children!

"What's the attraction with him?" I asked Prita, unable to believe it.

"I just love rich old men with grey hair," she

responded, giving me a teasing smile. "Sorry, Paul. You're just too young for me."

"And not rich enough!" I laughed and went off, shaking my head again.

Incredible! I knew these things went on, but whilst they might be shocking in some ways, they were to prove entirely trivial compared with what would happen later.

All was relatively quiet. I was covering the desk, amongst other things, for a few minutes while another staff member was attending to something. Les, the concierge, and I were chatting as we often did, whilst I chipped away at my checklist before drafting my report.

Just before 5.30am, a male called down to the desk from room 106, crying desperately, "Help! I need help urgently! My wife's coughing up blood!"

"We'll ring an ambulance, sir, and I'll be right up," I assured him, before putting down the phone.

"Les, call an ambulance immediately!" I said. "Room 106."

Then I rushed up to the room. As I approached the closed door, I could hear a male voice shouting from inside, "Karen! Karen!"

Knocking on the door, I heard one or two coughs, followed by a choking noise, and what sounded like the man talking to someone on the phone. I kept knocking on the door, harder now.

"Sir! Sir! It's the manager!" I called, but no one answered.

I hammered and called some more. It was no good. Cursing under my breath, I hurried back down to reception to check on the arrival time of the ambulance.

"Any sign?" I panted. Les shook his head.

Whilst I was at the desk, the man from 106 called again, to ask where the ambulance was. He was whimpering hysterically by now.

"Sorry, sir. We are still waiting for it. I will check."

He sobbed something indistinguishable. Something was evidently seriously wrong, so I called the emergency services again from my mobile to find out how much longer they would be, while I ran back up to the first floor again.

"They are on their way, sir," the dispatcher reassured me. "They should be with you soon. If you will hold the line for a moment, I will check with them now to see how far off they are."

As I approached the room this time, it was quiet. I knocked on the door, and it was opened straight away by the man, whose face was white and stricken with panic. He held his hands out in front of him, his fingers splayed, and I couldn't ignore the fact that they were covered in blood.

"Are you a medic?" he cried, his eyes wild with terror.

"No, but they're on their way," I told him, my mobile held to my ear. The emergency services operator was just speaking to the ambulance driver to get an accurate time of arrival.

"She's fucking dead!" the man shouted, his face distraught. "Get them here, NOW!"

The emergency services were still on the line, and on hearing this exchange, they started to give me instructions. "Go and see what the situation is. If you can perform some CPR in the meantime, that could help to save the woman's life until the paramedics can get there."

"OK," I said uncertainly as I pushed open the door that the guest was holding. "I have had some training, but..."

"Don't worry," the voice on the phone said calmly. "I'll talk you through it. Tell me when you're with her."

I followed the man into the room, and was appalled by what I saw. There was blood everywhere. I also noticed four empty wine bottles. It looked as if whatever incident had occurred had started in the bedroom, because there was a lot of blood spattered and smeared on one side of the bed, and a trail of fresh blood leading from there into the bathroom.

"In here!" said the man, and I went after him, inside the bathroom. The blood in here was worse still: pools of it, rich and red, and the metallic stench of coppery-iron filled the air.

A woman was lying on her back on the bathroom floor, her clothes and face covered in blood, and her long mousy-blonde hair was tangled and matted with it. It was clear that she was dying, if she wasn't dead already. Her eyes were wide open and staring. Her skin had a blue tinge to it, and her chest showed no sign of movement. I was horrified.

"We're here," I said into the phone, "I... I don't think she's breathing."

I quickly switched to speaker phone. The man had crouched over her body and started trying to give her CPR, although it was clear that he didn't know what he was doing. He was vaguely pressing her chest with his fingers, helplessly.

As the calm voice on the phone directed me, I started working on autopilot.

"Move away," I said. I immediately got down on the floor beside him to help. "If you can do the mouth-to-mouth when I say, I'll do the chest compressions."

As instructed over the phone, I checked her

airways, while the voice went on: "Place the heel of one hand near the end of her breastbone, in the centre of her chest."

"Right," I said.

"Place the heel of your other hand on top of that and interlock your fingers, but keep your fingers up, off the ribs."

My first aid training was coming back to me, but I didn't trust myself. I was relying on the voice like a programmed robot. I started applying chest compressions.

"You need to press down to a count of about two per second, or to the speed of the song *Staying Alive*."

"What?" I winced with the irony of it. Right then I couldn't have remembered a Bee Gees song to save my life. Or the woman's.

The voice on the line bizarrely started singing, "*Ah, ah, ah, ah, staying alive...* but don't worry, I'll count. You need to repeat this 30 times."

I listened to the voice on the phone as it counted with me and gently encouraged me. I felt bewildered – if I'd had to think for myself, I don't know if I would have been able to. I like to think I could. But I simply listened to the voice, and blocked out my own thoughts and panic, just concentrating on trying to get the woman breathing, or to keep her alive till help came.

"OK, carry on, but tell her husband to give her two rescue breaths. Tell him to pinch her nose closed. Take a deep breath and seal his lips around her mouth…"

"Did you get that?" I asked, hoping he had heard the amplified voice.

Her husband looked vague and blank. In shock, probably. I calmly repeated the instructions, still compressing, and stopped after 30. Her husband blew into her mouth until her chest rose, then stopped, allowing her chest to fall. He was to do this twice before I continued.

"Carry on giving 30 chest compressions followed by two rescue breaths until help arrives," the voice said. "You're doing fine."

"One – two – three – four," I cried, pumping beneath her breast bone with the heel of both hands, trying to see signs of life.

"That's it. Just keep that up," said the disembodied voice on the phone, soothingly.

"Where's the ambulance?" I panted. "Twenty-three – twenty-four…"

"On its way. Keep going… twenty-eight – twenty-nine – thirty! Rescue breaths, now."

I had to believe we were doing some good, but in the snatches I saw of the woman's face, in between her husband dipping down to gasp into her mouth, her eyes stayed open, dull and impassive.

Where are they? Where are they? I focused on pressing my hands down, rhythmically, watching the blood that was soaked into her thin jumper squeeze up between my fingers and under my nails. Was she alive? I couldn't tell, but I didn't want to stop. I couldn't stop. I became a machine, cutting myself off from the emotion and the horror of it all, just concentrating on counting and pressing down, endlessly. Time was lost to me. I was caught in a bubble of infinity, a nightmare; worse than a nightmare, because there was no escape.

After about five minutes, I was vaguely aware that back in the wider world, the first paramedic had arrived, looming over my shoulder and bobbing down into my peripheral vision. "OK, we'll take it from here," he said. "Well done."

I took my trembling fingers off the woman's chest, staring at the drying blood on them, and moved aside, vaguely. I still felt as if I had to count – one – two – three – four. I couldn't stop. Lives depended on it. Five – six – seven.

A second paramedic knelt down next to me. "Excuse me. Thanks."

I dragged myself out of the way, my arms aching, feeling sea-sick.

"She's still here," said the first. "Let's get a line in."

Still here? She's alive!

I stood up, giddy and disorientated like someone who has been on a long boat trip on rough waters, trying to adjust to the stability of land again, still feeling the steady tilt of movement, of rolling waves, even on the solid ground. I had the sensation that I was still doing chest compressions, over and over. I had a sense of disconnectedness, other-worldliness. My body was still working to the rhythm of CPR, the heels of my palms stinging with pressure and my limbs and heart still locked into the steady, persistent pattern of movement.

"Do you need me?" I asked weakly, gazing in wonder at my hands stained with blood, while the two paramedics swarmed over the dying woman.

"No," they both said. The male guest and I were ushered out of the bathroom while they worked on Karen.

"We're expecting more of our colleagues shortly," called the second paramedic. "Can you make sure they find their way?"

"Of course."

Feeling numb, I hurried back down to reception, but it wasn't long – seconds or a minute, time meant nothing to me – before two more medics arrived. I took them up to the room, and, remembering that I should keep senior management posted about serious incidents, I called Toby, the hotel manager, while the team were setting up their equipment in the bathroom, to inform him what was going on.

"Thanks, Paul. I'll come in straight away to provide assistance," he told me.

I soon got a call to say a fifth paramedic had arrived, and after dashing down to meet him, I accompanied him into the room. It was crowded with busy uniformed paramedics and their medical equipment and buzzing with muttered comments and louder requests. The activity in the bathroom seemed frantic.

"BP 83 over 60. We need more!" I heard one of the medics cry.

Someone had led Karen's stunned husband to the sofa, where he sat with his bloodstained hands balled up into fists. He was just staring into space.

I stood by, looking on helplessly.

Worryingly, the paramedics carried on working on Karen for an hour, trying to stabilise her. Finally they rang in to a hospital to say they were bringing her in. *Taking her in. That must be good… right? She must be well enough to travel. They've stabilised her. Right?*

Karen's husband seemed extremely calm, but that

was probably down to the fact that he was in shock.

As were we all. I was pacing the floor, filled with anxiety. *Did I do enough? Will she be OK?* The heels of my palms still seemed to be stinging with the pressure of pumping her chest. I could still see the ghastly spilt blood, her blue unresponsive face, smeared with blood – the whole scene imprinted on my mind. Everywhere I looked, the nightmarish images flashed into view.

But as long as she was alive, I had done something good.

When the medics were ready to leave the building, with the patient wrapped up in a red blanket on their trolley, I spoke to one of them to find out what was going on. I was rubbing the dried blood on my hands without even noticing, like a tic, like a habit. Unconscious. The dry blood flaked and peeled off with the friction, rolled into tiny black threads and dropped on the floor like nothing. Nothing at all.

"Is she going to be OK? What's happening now?"

The paramedic looked around warily, as if weighing up whether or not anyone would overhear him, and whether or not he should tell me. Eventually, he decided to come clean, and took an intake of breath.

"The patient is clinically dead," he said.

That was a punch to the gut, and it winded me. I swallowed hard, feeling dead myself. My ears started humming with the rush of blood, and I struggled to hear the rest of what he said, my hearing muffled.

"She lost so much blood, well… it was inevitable. She also has a medical history of cancer, her husband said."

I was in shock, too. I could have done more. I'd had her life in my hands. If I'd only been quicker. If I'd just got into the room earlier. If I had done something different… I wanted to faint. Run away. Something. But I had to continue working; be professional, carry on.

I focused on what I knew. What I had some control over. My job.

Les and I helped them to remove the medical equipment from the room. The medical team said they would return later to double check the room for "sharps", and that we should leave the room as it was, until it was given the all-clear to go in and clean up.

All-clear? What was this? A crime scene? What exactly had gone on there that night?

"Wash your hands, Paul," Les said quietly.

Coming back to consciousness, I realised I was just staring at my palms – still stained brown with blood in some areas, patchy flesh-coloured where I had rubbed it off. I don't know how long I had been looking at them, in a trance, gone mad, like Lady Macbeth.

I went to wash my hands, holding them under the tap, fascinated to see the amount of pale orangey-red bloody water that suddenly came from nowhere, flushing down the white basin. But somehow, I felt cleansed, more clear-headed.

Returning to the back office, I knew I was physically exhausted, but I was also still wired and full of adrenaline, and my mind was working overtime. What the hell had just happened?

I went over the facts as I knew them, trying to rationalise it all and make sense of what had just happened. I couldn't help but wonder why the man had called down to reception instead of dialling 999 straight away. We had acted as fast as we could, but if your wife was coughing up blood – especially *that* much blood – wouldn't your first instinct be to ring an ambulance directly? Not ring your hotel desk!

The whole thing was strange. Throughout the entire incident, there had been the odd brief outburst from Karen's partner, but he'd otherwise seemed very composed, even as they were taking her to hospital. If my partner had been dying - or dead - I can't imagine that I would have been even a fraction as calm as he was. Maybe it was shock, but who knows?

I tried to block them, but I couldn't stop those images flickering at the edge of my mind, insistent like flames trying to catch hold – her face, the blood. I had to cut off my feelings, forget, push it aside, get on – just to get through the next couple of hours.

"Get yourself home, Paul," said Toby. "You've had a shock."

"I'm fine," I said. I was lying. Just holding it all together. I carried on.

I finished my shift on auto-pilot, but when I got home, I fell to pieces. My world fell apart. I was lost. I entered a dark, dark, place and I wasn't sure I would ever get out of it. Truth be told, perhaps I never have.

I was signed off work and never went back to the Hotel Mannequin, but I couldn't bear it. The very thought of going back there triggered a breakdown. I can't tell you how many times I have gone over the incident; tried to make sense of it. Had the couple planned it all? Had she done something to herself? Taken something? Had he killed her, somehow? Was it the cancer? Was it just a terrible coincidence that she happened to die in our hotel that night? On my watch?

The post-mortem was inconclusive. That was no help. Could I have done more? Could I have done things differently?

I never recovered from that event. From the slick stickiness of the blood on my fingers, from the traumatic sights I saw, from the anxious feeling that I had been all that was keeping a human being alive, and I had failed. No matter what evidence there was to disprove it, I told myself she had died because of me. Because I wasn't good enough. Because I was incompetent. Dana had been right all along.

I still have flashbacks, even to this day. They are so real, they feel as if I am back there again: the sweating anxiety, the hot, trembling uselessness. The nightmares. Worst of all – the images. All of my senses are involved and over-stimulated. I am there again.

That final incident was the last straw. The trigger that set off the explosives that had been building up throughout my whole experience in that job. It blew my mind. It blew my world apart, in the end.

It started as the job you would love to do. Anyone would. I soon realised it was a job I hated, in so many respects – although I still loved the money. But that job took everything from me. I hate what it did.

I try to dissociate from it all. I dumb down my feelings. Feel numb. Feeling nothing. Better to feel nothing. But when you feel nothing in one area of your life, you tend to feel nothing in all the other areas too. Which is no way to develop relationships, to love, or to live life to the full.

I have been diagnosed with post-traumatic stress

disorder, which has affected my life in every way. My career. My relationships. My family. My mental health. My whole life.

As I said at the beginning, this story is mine to tell, although I never thought that my experience of working in a hotel would change my life forever. So pervasively. So damagingly. I thought it was going to be a dream job which would last a few short months, not a nightmare that would last me a lifetime.

What will come next? You just never know.